RESILIENCE

LIFE STORIES OF CENTENARIANS BORN IN THE YEAR OF REVOLUTION

PAUL
RICHARDSON
WRITER

NADYA
GREBENNIKOVA
WRITER

MIKHAIL
MORDASOV
PHOTOGRAPHER

Russian Life
BOOKS

Cover:
Photo of Yelizaveta Lakeyeva by Mikhail Mordasov.
Design by Vanessa Maynard.

ISBN 978-1-880100-54-7

Library of Congress Control Number: 2018900780

Russian Information Services, Inc.
PO Box 567
Montpelier, VT 05601-0567
www.russianlife.com
orders@russianlife.com
phone 802-223-4955

SPONSORED BY

AND OVER 300 CROWDFUNDING BACKERS

see list at back of book

ASSOCIATE PRODUCERS

Associate Producers

Alexei and Yuliya Bolshakov

CO-SPONSORS

Anonymous • Ricki Slattery Starrett

DIRECTORS

Harlan and Ellen Ratmeyer

The Centenarians' Current Homes

Showing the Borders of the Russian Empire in 1914

CONTENTS

INTRODUCTION

If you were born in Russia in January 1917, you could expect to live about 35 years.*

Of course, this is just an average. It does not take into account the fact that the country was suffering through the worst year of the worst war the world had ever known, that there was mass starvation and malnutrition on the home front, that the state of health care, law enforcement, and public safety were all abysmal by modern standards, or that Russian society was cleaving into countless slabs and slivers. And then there were the two major revolutions lying in wait for 1917.

Add to that the Spanish Flu outbreak, from which three million (over three percent of the population) died in Russia between 1918 and 1920, the Civil War (1918-1922), which claimed 10 million Russian lives, followed by the famines of 1921-1922 (five million deaths) and 1932-1933 (seven million deaths), dekulakization (6.5 million), the purges of 1937-38 (one to two million), and the utter devastation of the Second World War (26.6 million Soviet deaths between 1941 and 1945).

Such horrific numbers are impossible to grasp, and so it seems almost unbelievable that someone born in 1917 would have any chance of attaining their allotted, statistically average 35 years and survive until 1952. If they did, it would be an achievement of astonishing luck and will.

And yet a not insignificant number of individuals born within the bounds of the Russian Empire in 1917 achieved far more. They lived not just to 1952, but to 2017.

This, therefore, is a book about life, not death.

---

* This is just an estimate. A good figure for life expectancy in Russia in 1917 is hard to come by. But one scholar has estimated what it was in 1927, a decade later: 34 for men and 38 for women (E.Andreyev, L.Darski, T. Kharkova "Histoire démographique de la Russie. 1927–1959"). For the US in 1917, it was 52 for men, 56 for women. http://bit.ly/childrenof1917-intro

It is about people who vanquished all conceivable odds and have lived to be 100 – nearly three times their life expectancy at birth. This would be like a Russian born today living to be 200.

This is a book about what these remarkable people have seen and experienced, about how the passage of their lives – from childhood through marriage and old age – paralleled the life course of the country brought into the world in the year of their birth.

Each of their stories is very different, but all are stories of survival and endurance, of heart and courage, of the importance of hard work and good works, of family and community. Of resilience.

We had the inestimable honor of entering these people's homes, of being welcomed with open arms by their families. We supped with them and rifled through their family photos and memories. We disrupted their daily routines and re-arranged their furniture. We tried not to overstay our welcome, but also sought to steal every story they had strength and will to share.

This book is the product of these things and more. With it, we seek to transport you into these homes, into these lives, to be as moved by their stories as we were. Therefore, we have sought, as much as possible, to use the centenarians' own words to tell their stories, unfiltered. Their words appear as italicized paragraphs that are an integral part of each story.

In the end, we hope that we have done their stories justice, that you may come to know these remarkable individuals as we have, and that you, like us, will be changed by them.

Paul E. Richardson
Mikhail Mordasov
Nadezhda Grebennikova

p.s. A few notes about Russian words and historical terms. It is assumed that most readers are curious Russophiles and will know what is meant by a kolkhoz, a babushka, or perestroika, and that a gubernia or uyezd was an administrative district under the tsars, while now there are okrugs, krays and rayons.

For narrative simplicity, we have chosen not to footnote the many terms we feel most will be familiar with, while we have footnoted historical events and terms that may be less clear.

TATYANA SEMYONOVNA ORLOVA
NECHAYEVSHCHINA VILLAGE, TVER OBLAST
25 JANUARY 1917

Tatyana Orlova spends the summer in a little house on the banks of the Volga. To be more exact, on the banks of a small, complex sort of water object with gentle, sandy shores. It is actually several lakes, fluidly flowing one into the other. And straight through them, mixing with the lake waters, runs the mighty Volga River. Though, truth be told, in this region it is a very young, thin stream, more like a rivulet, actually.

This is Tatyana's home village, Nechayevshchina. It is a piece of ancient Russian land predating even ancient Muscovy, surrounded by dense forests and mosquito-infested bogs. Three plump fish on the region's coat of arms attest to the fact that this region is full of lakes. And here, into a typical peasant family on January 25, 1917, a little girl was born. And, since it was Tatyana's Day according to the Orthodox calendar, she was named Tatyana.

We had a very big family. Five children and grampa and grandma also lived with us. And we farmed. That means we sowed and mowed. And the children also worked. Everyone farmed.

I actually don't remember the revolution much. We lived peacefully before the revolution, like a family, quietly. Like a family unit. But with the revolution, a sort of persecution arrived. They took our cows. They did not allow the peasants who wanted to, to develop. Not to become exploiters, no, but simply to live for their family.

Take bread for instance. If a family had prepared bread for the coming winter, they came and opened the storage up and took everything. Yet our family, we had eight people. Tell me then, how is a peasant to survive? Even though he prepared this for his family through honest labor. They took the lock from his storage and took everything.

How can a child?... So the parents went at night, they dug a pit in the ground and put everything there, in order to hide just a bit of rye... In order not to die of hunger, in order to feed their kids. It was a sort of horror. And the children saw all of this, lived through all of this.

Today, you know, we are in sort of a similar period. They are now taking things by force, stealing. I don't understand. Why can't people do things honestly?

She begins her story suddenly, barely having greeted her guests, sitting in a white plastic chair in the shade of her wooden home. There is not a trace of embarrassment or confusion in her voice. It is as if the conversation had begun sometime before and she has now seized a moment to continue it. Tatyana has a powerful appearance, her chin held high. Yet her voice is soft, and her gaze is fixed, frozen on the horizon. Mentally, she is somewhere in the distant reaches of the past century.

We went to school, nearby, in Vseluki. There was a four-grade school there. It was two kilometers away. And everyone studied. Later, when the children started to grow up, Mama and Papa had this desire to somehow teach us more. Then they sent us to a seven-grade school in Peno. There my brother and I rented a small room and lived together. We studied in the fifth grade. And my older sister went to Leningrad at that time, and lived in the corner of some relatives' apartment; she did not have her own space.

After I finished fifth grade, I went to be with her, and started studying in the sixth grade in a Leningrad school. But, of course, we were very poor. She was a dressmaker and would stand in line until they gave her work.

*After finishing seventh grade, I entered the Leningrad Feldsher Obstetrics School.** *When I finished at the feldsher's school they sent me to Siberia. There I led a health center with a three-bed maternity home. By myself. It was a very big village. I had to decide everything on my own. There were so many difficulties. And after completing my two years there, I simply got out. Went on vacation and got out of there, because I simply could not stand it. Moved to Leningrad. In Leningrad I took courses to prepare for the institute. And for work. It was a really good situation, because I worked in a kindergarten. I got up very early, started seeing kids at seven, and worked until two, then went to my preparation courses.*

Tatyana did not succeed in entering the dental institute as she planned because the Soviet-Finnish War began. At the end of 1939 the Soviet Union invaded Finland, and, after three months of brutal losses, the sides signed a peace treaty. It was an infamous war, which cost the Soviet side dearly (it lost five times

---

* A *feldsher* is a primary care physician in a village who also can provide some emergency treatment, as well as obstetric and minor surgical care.

At Dispensary No. 19. Tatyana is the second from the left, standing.

Tatyana in her youth.

as many soldiers as its smaller neighbor) – in lives, money, and prestige, yet Finland ended up ceding over 10 percent of its territory, including lands along Lake Ladoga and in the Far North. What is more, it helped to decisively push Finland over to the side of Germany in the coming World War.

During the war, Tatyana worked as a nurse in a military hospital. One day she arrived at work and someone said to her, "Is that not your brother who just arrived? They are planning to amputate his legs; they were frostbitten."

There were 32 buildings, and I went from building to building, looking for him until I found him. He greeted me and, of course, was very surprised. It was something greater than happiness, of course, something you can't explain. He had lain in the snow for a long time. The snow was very deep that year. But thank God he kept his legs.

It's a good thing that the Finnish War was very short. So many youths were blinded, you can't even count them. The snow was so deep. They fell into the snow, and were shot at in the forest, and were blinded. They filled our buildings. And you know, these were people who were not, how do you say, in their right minds. Because to be blinded at the front is horrific.

And what about my brother? He was a pilot, a technician. Thank God his legs got better without amputation. They gave him six months off. He went to live with Mama and got better. Then he returned to service in his air unit. He said, "This war is not a war. There will be a war... a real war, and I don't know how it will end."

This brother, Pavel, disappeared without a trace during the first days of the Second World War, in July 1941. Her second brother, Alexei, died in November 1944 in a battle for a small Polish village that was at the time occupied by the Germans. Both of their names are on a cross that stands at the edge of Nechayevshchina.

Tatyana's parents, meanwhile, remained in the village during the war. Her father, Semyon, was the kolkhoz chairman. He is remembered in the family as a wise and decisive person. He was almost the only male left in the village and, though he was no longer young, he felt responsible for all the women and children who were left behind. The kolkhoz workers were supposed to continue working and give their harvest to the Soviet state. But, so that the village did not starve, he had to take some precautions.

What did Father do? He designated a group of women. But, of course, without telling anyone. They cleared some trees somewhere in the forest and planted wheat there. So that no one would know. And they did not tell anyone. And in the fall, when they reaped a big harvest, they divided it up among everyone in the whole village. Not only those who worked the plot, but the entire village. He plowed the land and put in beets. Those beets did not appear on any accounting sheet, and at the same time they were distributed by cart to all the women: they were fed, they saved children. And if one person had said something to someone, somewhere... But no one informed, no one.

The field remained a secret for many years. After the war ended, for his exemplary work as chairman of the kolkhoz, Semyon was given a special vacation at a sanatorium in the regional center. And teeth. All of the ones he had been born with had fallen out; they gave him a new set for free.

When you're standing at an operating table, you don't notice the face, the individual. You operate, and that's it. And afterward, you argue: should the amputation have been lower or higher? Our surgeons were always arguing. He would say, the arm should have been cut off higher." "No, lower," she would say, "you should cut off less because he's going to go on living." And the surgeon would say, "But it needs to be higher, or else there will be gangrene." So, they really didn't pay close attention to all that... And how could you, really? Tell me how?

When you are standing at an operating table, you don't notice the face, the individual.

There was a lot of hunger on the Leningrad front. And not only Leningrad was starving. The whole army was too. And they dropped rusks and herring from the planes. And when they tossed them from the planes, all the soldiers were ready to die just to get a little piece, a packet, to gulp it down. And when we washed them, we did not distinguish who was who, man or woman. They were all just bones. The bones and pelvis stuck out on all of them. So much was wasted, so many were hungry on the front. And not only Leningrad.

Working on the front lines, I got a vitamin deficiency. Total deficiency. Operating once for 36 hours, standing at the operating table, my legs became swollen. I couldn't move. And I lay in the hospital for six months. They fixed me up there...

And operations, oh how the operations went. You know, they went one after another like a conveyor. Oy, Lord, there was some of everything. Today I have forgotten all of that, as if it were part of an ordinary life...

Tatyana received a medal "For Courage." Under artillery fire, at risk to herself, she pulled 13 wounded soldiers from the field. Three of them were in critical condition, but she succeeded in giving them medical aid and saving their lives.

She traveled with the troops to Poland and then returned home to her parents victorious, and pregnant. Her daughter Valentina was born, her only child, and she went to work in the village hospital, located on the opposite side of the river. It was built at the beginning of the twentieth century, yet it still stands today: a few dark, wooden buildings sinking into the earth amid a dry pine forest. Only now it also contains a home for the elderly.

Tatyana worked there for eight years, running back and forth every day across a dam that spanned the lake. She says she can't remember ever returning home at six o'clock in the evening, that is working normal hours. But she does

Parking in Peno village, near Nechayevshchina.

Monument to those who fell in World War II, Gora village, near the hospital where Tatyana worked, and across the river from Nechayevshchina.

remember how quite often she would arrive home from work and her mother would say, "Run back, the hospital phoned; they need you."

When the dam was removed, it became very difficult to get to and from the hospital, so Tatyana started thinking about leaving the village. Her father supported her, saying she should move to Leningrad.

He was a very far-sighted person. He said to me, "You need to get a better situation, to get out of here." But it was also not very easy there, you know, not easy in the city. I bought a place, a kind of veranda. Sort of a cold bit attached to a building, like a kitchen. Very cheap. I think we lived there for over 20 years, then we received an apartment.

She worked in a venereological dispensary, and says that back in those days things were far more orderly than in modern hospitals. The reason, she says, was people's true patriotism – a willingness to work in good faith, conscientiously.

I am a person, you might say, who is not a gadabout. I am not a great lover of crowds. I mostly loved to work. Oy, I didn't have anything to rejoice about. I don't know, I don't remember that I celebrated anything. What was there to celebrate when I had such low pay and no apartment? I work in the dispensary, and I go to a thread factory – I was on night duty there. Work the night shift, then go to work. That's it – working nonstop I didn't notice if there were any happy days. There were days when I got enough sleep. Yes, getting enough sleep was good. At least I was rested. But otherwise, there were no happy days... Yes! My daughter, true enough, was well educated. I have constantly received thanks for her upbringing, she was very advanced.

Tatyana readily admits, however, that she did not give enough time to her daughter Valentina. After all, she had to raise her alone. But she did everything so that she got a good education. And Valentina in turn did all she could so that her own son studied in good schools and at a prestigious university. To this day, Tatyana and Valentina live in Petersburg and spend their summers in their village along the Volga.

In the end, this centenarian feels that the secret to her long life is her enthusiasm for work.

I really loved people. Wounded, sick. I gave them my soul.

Valentina adds that her mother did not have any harmful habits. She never liked alcohol, though she might drink a small glass on a special occasion. She also always read a lot – books and newspapers – and was never idle. If she were at home and sat down to watch the television, she would pick up something to sew or knit.

And she has always been distinguished by her great interest in life and her ability to overcome difficulties. For example, Valentina recalls how, when things became difficult with foodstuffs in the 1980s, when things were being sold on ration coupons and one had to stand in line for hours, Tatyana commented, surprised, "Is this what you call hunger? But we have ration coupons."

When there are difficult times, she simply says, "This too we'll survive."

Tatyana's daughter Valentina gathered funds for the cross that stands at the entrance to Nechayevshchina.

NIKOLAI PAVLOVICH TRESKIN

IRKUTSK

4 MARCH 1917

Scientists should study the DNA of Nikolai Pavlovich Treskin. He turned 100 in March of 2017, but looks not a day over 70. His grandfather lived to be 100, and his great-grandfather 110.

Nikolai shuffles around the large garden behind his daughter's home, with the slight help of a cane, stopping to sit for a while on a bench or to breathe in the warm afternoon air. He has a stillness about him, a calm that makes it seem nothing could perturb him and nothing ever has. All business.

"Ask me questions and I will answer," he says matter-of-factly. And then he delivers dry, almost staccato answers to the questions. But, as the interview continues, he warms and offers longer, more discursive replies.

Dressed in a bright blue dress shirt and a sheepskin-lined vest, he dons a cap when he sits in the shade, but takes it off for the filmed interview.

His daughter, Lyudmila, seems a bit put out by the whole situation. Repeated requests to move the interview indoors – in light of the fact that the home is on the flight path of Irkutsk International Airport and a tram runs right in front of the house – fall on deaf ears. "This will be fine," she says, insisting on offering sweets and tea beneath an arbor, but refusing to have her photo taken under any circumstances.

Beyond Nikolai, halfway back in the garden, a small fountain burbles and bubbles. Butterflies flit between colorful flowers. A plane roars overhead.

I was born in the village. Talyany settlement, Bokhan Rayon. I lived there until I was seven. At seven they brought me to the city. And to this day I have lived in the city. I had my own home, no worse than my daughter's. Yes. Then my wife died, and my

daughter brought me here. I sold the home and now I live with her. I live very well. I have a very fine granddaughter. And my grandchildren are all very good, generally speaking. They all have higher education. So, what else you want to know?

His speech is simple, direct, uncomplicated, and rather soft. Not brusque so much as quietly terse. But as questions are added, layers of the onion are peeled back. It turns out that much of Nikolai's life turned on a sad, accidental event when he was four.

Mother and Father were peasants. Father was murdered by bandits... I was just four.

Later exposition of the story reveals that his father was ambushed by anti-communist thugs while walking alone outside their village, apparently mistaken for someone else. "He wasn't even a communist," Nikolai says. "They just killed him and that was it."

Still, he somehow remembers the good times in the village before the family moved to Irkutsk.

We had two homes. A river flowed nearby. We swam. We lived fairly well in the village. But when they killed Father, that is when everything began. Mother was very young... Then she got married. Sold off the farm. Went to the placer mine and returned with nothing. No farm, nothing remained... Then she married again, this time successfully... He was a shoemaker. But he was an Austrian. A good shoemaker he was, and we started to live well again. There was enough of everything...

He was much older than Mother. Educated. Knew lots of languages... He was very cultured and taught me too. And then we moved to Irkutsk. I was seven when they brought me here... And when they started dekulakizing and putting non-Russians in prison, this was in 1937, he was gone for a whole year [to live and work in Bodaybo†]... When he returned, he never left... He was about 90 when he died.*

But his stepfather was not simply a clever, cultured, Austrian-born shoemaker. He could also be abusive and dangerous.

He was very strict. Drunk, he was so weak anyone could hit him. But sober, keep away. I was afraid of him from when I was very small. If you, say, stupidly sharpened your pencil with his knife, and even washed and wiped it, he'd still somehow find out. That was all it took.

In 1934, Nikolai graduated from a technical school, having trained to be an auto mechanic.

---

* Actually, dekulakization was earlier. 1937 was the time of show trials and repression of anyone with any sort of foreign ties, among other trumped-up charges.

† A town about 1100 kilometers from Irkutsk.

I just had four years of school. Didn't have any memory. To this day I don't have a good memory. My sister, she got lucky that way. She graduated from two technical schools, and from the teachers' institute. Everything was easy for her... And me, I would memorize my multiplication tables at night and by morning they were forgotten. That's what my memory was like as a child. I worked...

I worked for a long time as a mechanic. Then as a carburetor man, repairing carburetors, and lastly, I painted cars. They paid well for painting cars. I always lived pretty well.

The happiest time in his life, Nikolai says, was in 1938, when he met and married his first wife, Maria.

We lived in the same building. I lived downstairs, she lived upstairs. We basically grew up together. And, well, we liked each other and got married. She had a heart condition. Her mother did as well... So she died prematurely. Fell asleep and didn't wake up.

But I lived with my second wife a long time. She died when she was 82, 12 years ago already.

But that was after the war. Married in 1938, Nikolai got a draft deferment for a year. The young couple had a child and then, in 1939, Nikolai was sent off to serve in Mongolia. He remembers the locals only with scorn.

The Mongols are a dirty people. One of theirs hasn't even died yet and they haul them away... Their gods... if a dog has a red ribbon tied to it, it means he is a god. If a camel has red on its hump, it means it too is a god, no harming it. That's it.

He was still serving his term in the army when the war began. And then, in 1943, he was sent to Beloostrov, near Leningrad, to serve as a sapper, laying and defusing mines around the blockaded city.

Okh, Leningrad was... If only you'd seen what went on there. Horrors. The attics were filled with corpses. There, on Fontanka [Canal]... when it started to thaw, you'd see an arm, a leg. Horror... Leningrad suffered so much...

Okh, Leningrad... If only you'd seen what went on there. Horrors.

But no sooner had the war ended and again Leningrad – they are such good people, again it started getting cleaned up. There, if some guy is walking along the street smoking and tosses aside a cigarette, someone will yell at him, "Pick up your cigarette!" That's the sort of laws they have. Everywhere it's clean and orderly... Well, it was, now they say it's changed. I haven't been in Leningrad for a long time. The people are very nice, Leningraders, pure Leningraders. Gentle. Not like in Moscow. There, if a person is walking, looking for some street or other and asks for help. ...[In Leningrad] any man or woman will stop and give advice on how to get there. But not in Moscow. If they like the looks of you, they will talk to you. But if not: "I'm not the information bureau!" and walk away. [laughs] Right there, that's the difference between Muscovites and Leningraders.

Nikolai at a public demonstation. He is third from the left, in the fedora.

Nikolai then and now. At left, a photo that he sent to this daughter Lyudmila in June 1946. At right, Nikolai in his Irkutsk backyard garden.

These good feelings come from the time Nikolai spent in Leningrad after the war. He was posted there until 1946, defusing mines, and speaks at length on the superior qualities of German versus Russian mines, such that one is in awe that he or any other sapper survived five years of handling them. But, as to the Germans themselves, he is not as impressed.

[The Germans] they did not consider how large Russia is. For the Germans to take Russia, they would have had to fight to every corner of the oblast, and then there is still plenty of the country left. Russia is an immense country. There is so much land.

Demobilized in 1948, Nikolai traveled home to Irkutsk and walked into his home one night as if he were just returning from work for the day. His wife fainted, as she had not expected him. He had, after all, been away for nine years.

Nikolai went back to work as a mechanic, working in the motor pool of Glavsevmorput.*

They took barges up the Lena [River], then from the Lena to the North... It was a very rich organization. They had everything. Not a cafeteria, but a buffet – whatever you like. And very cheap. Drivers and mechanics got good work clothes. It was a very exclusive car depot...

I was always on the board of honor wherever I worked. And often got bonuses...

In 1953, the day Stalin died, Nikolai happened to be in Yakutia.

Many people were sent to Yakutia. And many were there who had served out their sentences. When Stalin died, they put on such a drinking party – they celebrated the fact that Stalin died. Yes, well, of course, not everyone, but the majority. Almost everyone there was like that...

Many, many [were put in prison under Stalin]. And innocents were convicted. Completely. There were troikas.† Troikas, they judged. I get upset at you once, and that's it [you are convicted]. Completely innocent of anything and everything. So many people suffered. They conducted investigations badly. If someone writes something about me, there should be a chance to meet them face to face, so that they have to say it to my face. But back then, there was nothing like that. Once and done. Things were bad then... Many innocent people disappeared. In exile and everywhere.

Under Khrushchev, there were other issues.

Khrushchev did not have what you call a great mind. He did a lot of things, he did, that Khrushchev. Back then, kolzhoz farmers who had three or four cows were decreed to be allowed just one. Despite the fact that they had seven children. So there

---

* The Soviet organization (1932-1964) in charge of the Northern Sea Route – from Vladivostok around the top of Russia, and to Europe through the Arctic.

† Three-person judicial bodies that meted out immediate and un-appealable sentences.

The Angara River as seen from the Taltsy Ethnological Museum, between Irkutsk and Lake Baikal.

was that sort of thing. Forbade everything, including keeping pigs. Khrushchev did plenty that was bad.

And, as to the 1990s?

Perestroika? Well, some things were good, some were bad under perestroika. Much was lost with perestroika. They needed to reform things entirely differently. They should have immediately introduced discipline. It's all a matter of leadership. Just like in a family – if the father and mother are good, the children will be too...

[Yet] somehow I never lived badly... others of course suffered... When there were ration cards, of course, it was bad. Back then a loaf of bread cost 200 rubles, and prices were high... The people, of course, have endured plenty. But now everyone lives well in Irkutsk.

Looking back, when pressed, he says that Lenin was probably the best of the Russian leaders in the 100 years he witnessed. Until the current leader, that is.

Well, now we have the excellent Putin, everyone respects him. If there had right away been a person like this, everything would have been different [in the Soviet era]. Putin's word is his bond. If he says something, promises it, then everything will be ok.

For his part, Nikolai says that his secret to long life is simple:

The first thing is smoking. I have never smoked. The second is vodka. He who does not drink vodka and does not smoke, he will live long.

Even in the war, he says, when soldiers were given 12 packs of tobacco a month, he would give all of his packs out to his troops.

And, despite working under rather difficult conditions (years cleaning carburetors with gasoline and painting cars with toxic paint), he still looks far younger than his years.

Others say I that I am just 70. They don't believe me [that I am 100]. They say I tacked on some years.

The backyard garden at Lyudmila and Nikolai's home, where Nikolai sits and strolls on warmer days.

LIDIYA NIKOLAYEVNA MOTINA
SAMARA
12 MARCH 1917

The value of a project designed to capture memories and history becomes crystal clear when it confronts a situation where there is little left to capture. When memories are not shared, they pass away with the mind they inhabited. When unique documentary sources are lost, it is as if the history they carried never happened.

Lidiya Motina was an only child. Her parents were small-scale manufacturers who had a shop on the first floor of a building in downtown Samara, on what was originally Ural Street, but which in 1934 was renamed Brothers Korostelyovykh, after two local brothers who embraced the revolutionary cause, one of whom died early from overwork and bad health, the other who was tried and executed on trumped up charges in 1937.

A small woman with a soft, barely audible voice, Lidiya is gripped by dementia and memory loss. Her eyes shine not with wonder and curiosity, but with fear and confusion. She sometimes does not recognize her own daughter, and frequently gets disoriented. "What room is this?" she asked her daughter Tatyana recently. "That is the toilet," Tatyana replies. The apartment, which is uncluttered and echoes with the emptiness of a space ready to be put up for sale, is suffused with the odor of urine.

The memory loss began three years ago, Tatyana explains, when Lidiya fell and broke her arm at home. "She does not go outside any longer," Tatyana says.

"I don't allow her. Because she said to me one time, 'You know, I stopped and looked around and thought, this is not my house. I did not know where I was. And then I looked and saw the rocket. Ah, that's where I am. I live near the

Above, the family of Lidiya's mother Anna, who stands behind her mother, with a white bow in her hair. Below left, Lidiya as a young girl. Below right, her mother and father (standing) at their downtown shop.

rocket.'* After that, I said to her, 'Mama, don't go out alone.' And now for three years, she has not gone out at all. She was about 97, I think, when I forbade her. But when I go walking with her, it's fine... Up until 97, she went everywhere, to the stores, alone, doing as she liked. But now we cook everything and bring it to her. We heat things up. She stopped cooking long ago. I stopped letting her do that."

But it is not merely the broken arm that Tatyana thinks is at the root of her mother's memory loss.

"She lives alone. Previously, neighbors visited her. But all her neighbors have died, you understand? Because of that, she has very limited interactions... And I can say with complete confidence that if she was living in a family, she would be more active. Because she was always very active. She never sat at home, she and Papa were always on trains, whenever I remember them. They would leave me with my babushka... and go to Crimea, the Caucasus. They went and traveled everywhere, never sat at home..."

But there is no family alternative. Tatyana is Lidiya's only daughter, and her own living conditions – her husband is very sick – don't allow her to take her mother in. She also has not considered whether a social worker could be brought in to help. "I have not looked into this," she says. "I just don't have any additional capacity. My husband – he is an invalid – and I have just spent four months getting his official status worked out... I've had no time to deal with this, no matter if money, even just kopeks, is involved. What is, will be. What is, will be..."

So she stops by once or twice a day to check on her mother, to make sure everything is okay. And to lock her in at night. Which she has had to do since a few months ago, when Lidiya started waking up neighbors in the early morning hours.

But, of course, life was not always like this. Lidiya's father, Nikolai, was one of the original builders of Samara's important Maslennikov Factory – ZIM (also known as Factory No. 42), which made Katyusha rocket launcher shells and, later, Pobeda ("Victory") watches. It existed for nearly 100 years and was a major enterprise in the city, but it barely lasted to the end of the Soviet Union, and was shuttered in 1990.

After finishing nine years of schooling, including at the Institute of Planning, Lidiya worked at ZIM, eventually becoming the head of a department.

---

* Throughout the Soviet era, Samara/Kuybyshev was notable for its rocket production, among other things. All of the Soviet cosmonauts were sent into space using R-7 rockets built in Samara. Lidiya was referring to a rocket monument.

Married in 1941, she avers that she has no memory of her husband Boris.

How can I remember that? It was so long ago.

Her replies to all questions are similar.

What is her normal day like?

It goes by. You try not to forget yourself.

The same year she was married, in 1941, her father died at just 45 years old, from a heart attack, likely because the ambulance did not arrive quickly enough, Tatyana says.

At that time, Samara was actually known as Kuybyshev, named for Politburo member and Stalin acolyte Valerian Kuybyshev, who died at his desk of a thrombosis in 1935. As Moscow became threatened, the city, which was already the destination for a huge number of evacuated factories, became the site of the government in evacuation, including the Supreme Soviet, most major foreign diplomatic representations, and the Bolshoi Theater. Notably, it was in Kuybyshev in March 1942 that Shostakovich's memorable Seventh Symphony ("Leningrad") was premiered.

Lidiya's first child, a little girl Natalya, died at two and a half months, in 1942, after being infected with sepsis at the hospital. Lidiya and her husband worked in the factory throughout the war, and Tatyana was born in 1945, the year the war ended. She grew up an only child.

"I lived here until I was 26. With them, but not in this apartment. In the house on Lunacharsky street. Then I married and went off to Moscow. But I

Lidiya with her husband Boris in November 1950.

Lidiya's mother Anna.

Lidiya in 1937, center, while a student at the Institute of Planning.

Lidiya with her granddaughter Svetlana and her great grandson.

did not like living in Moscow. I don't know why. I lived there three years and returned here. I said to my husband, 'If you want, you can come with me; if you don't want to...' That's how it was. And his father, my husband's, he was an advisor to Suslov."*

Tatyana displays a photo of her mother and family from the pre-revolutionary era (page 32). "It's a very interesting photo, one of just a few," she says.

"There were a lot of photos that Mama did not bring with her when they moved here 20 years ago, when they were given this apartment... All those old photos, Mama forgot about them, and I was living in Moscow at the time. So it is very sad, very sad. It was such an amazing album. I said to Mama, 'Why didn't you take them?' 'I forgot.' They were in the building when it was torn down...

"It's very sad. They were such good photographs. Yesterday I called my cousin, and I said, 'Lyub, have you kept your babushka's photographs?' They have moved five times from place to place. And nothing is left, everything has been lost, for the most part. And of all our family, we are the only ones of that era who remain, who can remember anything. Or can more or less still remember. That's how it is. What else can be said?"

---

* Mikhail Suslov (1902-1982), known as the "grey cardinal" of the Kremlin, was a longtime Party Secretary who rose to power under Stalin, was influential under Khrushchev, and whose career peaked in the Brezhnev era. He was a member of the Politburo from 1952-53 and again from 1955-1982. He was born into a peasant family in Saratov Gubernia.

MARIA PETROVNA KONYAYEVA

KOLOMNA, MOSCOW OBLAST

15 MARCH 1917

Maria Konyayeva sits patiently on the divan, dressed in a long, maroon-colored dress, anxious to share her stories. Almost entirely deaf, she clutches a folder with papers that she wants to share, while her daughter and son-in-law talk at length with journalists beyond the range of her hearing.

When she does finally begin speaking, it is in a soft, slow cadence that is at once breathless and measured; there seem to be no hard consonants in her repertoire. At times she struggles to force out a syllable, her voice skittering and hoarse. She laughs easily and lightly, often marveling at the amazing "clan" she has accumulated.

She also needs to look directly into the eyes of her interlocutor when she is talking. She is making a connection; break her gaze and her story trails off. If you are not looking, you are not listening...

Born in the village of Ilyinskoye, southeast of Moscow, Maria was the last of seven children (and the only girl). She was orphaned at 13, when her mother died. Her father had died eight years earlier, but she has memories of him from the time near the end of the Civil War.

I remember him, eh, I was about five years old. There were maneuvers in '22. Nearby, through the village next to our home. I ran out to take a look, and he, Papa, went out. For some reason he had a limp, I don't know why. He was in valenki, sick. Yes. And I stood there for a long time. That is an episode I remember about Papa. But I don't remember anything else about him. No, wait, I do remember one other. My brothers, he cajoled them with a whip [laughs]. But other than that, nothing, I don't remember anything about Papa.

Maria's parents and brothers.

Above, Maria, center, in white blouse, always loved outdoor sports. Below left, Maria as a young woman. Below right, skiing at about the same age (she is on left).

But Mama was sick for a long time. And I had to heat the stove by myself. And I, I baked bread. I was 13. Either I under-salted it or over-salted it. Well, she lay there, and what she was sick from, I don't know. She lay there and never complained. Didn't ask me for anything. We lived simply then, and, well, I made her kasha, she ate millet kasha. And on the day she died, she called me over from the stove, "Don't make kasha for me today." So I didn't make it, I went to the stove and I heard her cry out, "Aaa," and that was it. I ran over to her, kneeled right on the bed, crying, "Mama, Mama!" But she only answered, she answered me: "Aaa... Aaaa," and that was it. And I... Oy, I remember so much. I had to live through so much, so much...

She had just four years of education, and had to take work for a time as a nanny, doing "whatever was asked" of her.

You go where they shove you. And so I unlearned how to laugh. I never laughed... Why laugh when all there was were tears?

A cousin stepped in and got her enrolled at a technical school in the town of Ozyory, southeast of Moscow. But Maria gave it up in 1936 when she had to go back to Ilyinskoye to get her passport, then got a job working in a bread factory in Kolomna, where she worked until 1939, and where she has lived ever since.

It was in Kolomna in 1939 that she met her husband, Vasily, when attending a dance with a friend. He worked as an engineer at a gramophone factory.

He asked, "Can I walk you home?"

"As you like. Let's go. I'm not going to put you in my pocket in any case..." [laughs]

We went together for three months... very properly, very correctly. He was a very good husband to me, and all my friends liked him. First of all, he did not drink, he was not a drunk. Of course, he had a little drink on holidays or some anniversaries... He never swore at me and I lived with him for 53 years. We celebrated our golden anniversary. He was a very good husband..."

Did you fall in love with him right away?

Well, what do you mean? I don't know. It was fine. I liked him. He looked after himself, was clean... He did not paw at me.

Do you recall how he proposed?

Well, he said to me, "I want to get married on the October Revolution anniversary [November 7, 1939], are you game?"

And I said, "Oh, you."

And he said, "What do you mean, 'Oh, you'? Say yes or no!" [laughs]

So, he put on the wedding, and all of his relatives were there...

When the war came, Kolomna was mostly evacuated in advance of the German assault, but the city was never taken. The Germans were halted a few dozen kilometers west and Kolomna became a main gathering point for artillery units. All the local factories were turned into ammunition plants.

Vasily was put in charge of running a department at one such factory. An extremely resourceful, inventive engineer (who put his name on some 120 inventions), he had just seven years education, but made up for it by working long hours overseeing the factory's production of war material. Maria, meanwhile, stayed at home. The couple's first child, Larisa, was born in 1940, and a boy, Yuri, was born in 1941.

I was pregnant with the little boy. And at that time my mother-in-law and father-in-law, their family, they also lived in Kolomna, and they had some cattle, a cow they had. And they asked me and another daughter-in-law to go to the riverbank, across the bridge, and cut some cabbage stumps for it. Well, we went. We never could refuse anything they asked, never.

So we get there, and we are cutting away at them, Polina with an axe, and me gathering them up. I looked up and saw a plane flying from the direction of the iron bridge, so low, it was almost impossible. I raise my head and it is flying directly at us. And I see what is painted on it: German. I look at him, and he looks at me, the pilot... And at that moment, Lord, Lord God, Polina dropped the axe and it fell on my foot. And I fell down and I knocked Polina over. And he started shooting, shooting: ta-ta-ta-ta-ta-ta... I saw the machine gun, but he was already turning away... flying just as low... He flew and flew... and nearby was the factory where they made ships. And this factory was formerly owned by Germans. And everyone said that was why they didn't touch it; the factory was never bombed.

I raise my head and it is flying directly at us. And I look at what is painted on it: German.

Yuri lived just seven months. "He died in infancy," says Galina, Maria's second daughter (born in 1944). "There was nothing to feed him. They were left all but alone by the evacuation. There was no milk, no doctors, nothing."

Explaining what her father was like, Galina recounts how "once he was given a task by the military to prepare some sort of ammunition. He worked at it for two days straight. He didn't know how to draft, nothing like that, he did it all in his head. He created a die that, without turning on a lathe, was exact to the millimeter. They used this to stamp out the ammunition... He had such a brain. He always said to me, 'Daughter, if only I were literate, I could have...'"

He was an excellent person, didn't drink, never swore at me. Never, 53 years, he never in his life swore at me, never raised his voice, no how.

"Our family was very lucky," Galina says. "Father was a very positive influence, he never drank, never fooled around, never smoked, there was none of that. And their example helped us raise our children because they saw all of

Maria poses before a wall mural in her family's apartment.

this. And they too grew up to be very positive people... There were no stresses, no divorces, no fights, no scandals. Our family had none of that."

In my clan, there are no lazy people. There are none who would say, "I don't want to, I'm not going." That's just the normal way with us.

When Galina was six or seven, she fell ill, was misdiagnosed with tuberculosis, and spent a year immobilized in a tuberculosis ward trussed up in a full body cast. When she was finally "cured" and a threat of diphtheria arose, Maria was given the chance to take her daughter home, so that she could be isolated. She jumped at the chance and dedicated herself to healing her daughter, teaching her to walk again, helping her build up her strength in the difficult post-war years.

When she got sick, I bought a goat, so that there would be milk... We lived on the banks of the Moscow River... I tied her down across the bridge and she'd eat all day. And at dinnertime, I'd go over and milk her, and I took Galya along, with a teapot. And she would drink it up, milk her, drink some more. Oh, how that goat saved us...

"No one else drank goat's milk but me," Galina says. "Goat's milk, cocoa, and salo. They put my legs in hot water with nettles. Refused to see doctors."

Galina got better and went on to receive a higher education, graduated from two institutes, and became a physics teacher. Her older sister, Larisa, completed graduate school and was well on her way to becoming an academician when Chernobyl struck.*

They lived in Mogilev [in Belarus], and the radiation fell there. And she, she had a dacha and was always messing around in the dirt there with her hands. That played a part, likely. She died.

"She was teaching at an institute in Mogilev," Galina adds. "There was a first of May demonstration, and they didn't say anything to anyone about it [Chernobyl]. She went, and at that time the radiation cloud was above them."

Larisa died in 1991, of stomach cancer. And her father, Maria's husband, died a year later. "My father went to them [Larisa's] to help them out at the dacha, to collect up the radioactive dust," Galina says. "They thought that it could be gathered up. And he got himself a dose... And then he got the same diagnosis, and died a year after her."

There is a tendency for the stories of centenarians to focus overly much on tragedy. Because those are the starkest, most searing memories, and they bubble to the surface with a ferocity that everyday life cannot match. But that does not mean that life has been filled only with sadness.

---

* April 26, 1986.

In fact, Maria was active all her life, working as the monitor of a gas boiler.

I got a lot of reading done, because all I had to do was sit and watch the machinery.

In her free time, she and her husband loved to ski and skate. But they left Kolomna only rarely, and Maria barely remembers vacations at nearby sanatoria, though she does share fond memories of two stays at special camps that allowed Galina to heal while continuing her schooling.

Still, over the last decade – in her nineties – Maria began to be hit by health problems. Seven or eight years ago she suffered two heart attacks in two years. Yet she answered it with her typical composure.

After the second one, I could no longer walk... My grandchildren and daughter got me a wheelchair...

Maybe God likes me. He doesn't want to let me go.

Her son-in-law, Yevgeny, whom Maria can't praise highly enough for his kindnesses, breaks in. "Can I add something? When she was recovering from her second heart attack, the doctor said they couldn't save her. But they did, they brought her back to life, and a week later the doctor stopped by to examine her. She takes his hand and says, 'I have prepared a *chastushka* for you.' And she recites her poem:

'I would sing, I would sing, I would have some fun.
'But I am old, and sick, and now for my doctor I've fallen.'"

And of course you can't have just one *chastushka*, so after Yevgeny finishes with his story, Maria offers another:

Oh, you, deck, deck,
You rock me.
And my century, my deck,
*Crashes into the pier.**

When asked what it takes to live to be 100, Maria replies with equal shares of wonder and wisdom.

I myself am surprised that I have lived so long. Only God knows why. I don't. I didn't give food much attention, nothing. I don't know. Maybe God likes me. He doesn't want to let me go...

Oh, who am I to advise? Be less angry. [laughs] Be good to everyone. Don't flee work... Up until I was 100, I had no understanding of what it meant to lie about

* Not her creation, but her re-make of a famous song, in which she replaces the words "my sorrow" with "my century."

in the daytime and do nothing, or to rest. Once a neighbor said to me, "Marusya, I don't know how you do it, when you walk you just skip and go faster, faster, faster"...

I have always been moving, moving, moving...

Does she have any regrets?

What is there to regret? If something should or was supposed to happen, that's what happened.

LEOPOLD DAMIECKI
CHODKOWO-KUCHNY, POLAND
19 MARCH, 1917

During the twentieth century, life in Poland – historically the doormat for European militaries – was not conducive to longevity. With a population of around 25 million in 1900, it rose to 35 million on the eve of the Second World War (after some painful decreases during and after WWI), then fell to below 24 million, not to recover to its prewar levels until the mid-1970s. Of the three million Jews in Poland in 1939, less than one in ten survived the war and death camps. During and after the war, some 7 million ethnic Germans fled the country.

Yet if you were resolved to remain in this country wracked by a century of war, emigrations, genocide, deportations, and Communism, there are probably few professions that would have offered greater personal security than that of butcher.

Leopold Damiecki hardly fits what might be the stereotypical image of the beefy, broad-shouldered butcher. Small and trim, but also very vibrant and lively, he is quick to note that all his life he has loved music and the good life.

I did not like studying very much, but I liked music and theater. I was part of every school play, I played in school orchestras. Things like books did not interest me very much.

It does not take much coaxing to get him to bring out his trumpet (or an aged, foot-pumped accordion) and impress visitors with a few tunes. When asked what is the secret to living to 100, he has a ready answer:

Everybody keeps asking me about that secret. Once a pharmacist asked me for some kind of longevity program. And I told her: "Pani magister, [a Polish honorific for pharmacists], you need to eat well, help yourself to vodka sometimes, and from

Above, Leopold at 14, front row, right.

Left, Leopold holding his daughter Janna (left) and one of her friends.

time to time have relations with women." ...I only eat fatty meat. People say it's not good for you, but I have absolutely no taste for lean meat! To this day, I like fatty meats better. And I like to drink a little vodka sometimes. When I was thirty or forty, I drank it quite a bit.

Born in the village of Bobino Wielkie, Leopold was the child of middling peasants.

It was a hard life. Sometimes there was not even any bread. Before the war, there was lots of poverty. But not for everyone...

It was really bad before the war. There were a lot of poor people with satchels going around, begging. No one locked the doors in warm weather. Today there's no poverty like this. The state gives everyone something. It's pennies, but every old and infirm person has something...

I had a good childhood when I was still going to school. I was part of school orchestras, theater clubs, and, when I was outside, all I did was graze cows. Such was rural life. Not too fun.

What can I say about my parents? They'd beat my ass hard with a belt. My father thrashed me and told me to graze the cows. When I got them back, I wanted to steal apples from a neighbor, but I never did because I was afraid. My classmates did.

Later, I would work for other people during the fall, dig up their plots, and people would get together and ask others to come, women too, and together everyone would dig potatoes, then later have parties with music and dancing. Such were the digging parties. Back then, my brother and I would play the drums.

That was our life, not bad, but not too good. If you didn't die before your time, that was nice...

I remember that before the war some had it bad, some had it good, just like today. But it wasn't good. Now it's better. Much better than before the war. In Communist times, not everyone had it good, too: only the ones who ran things. Regular people who weren't communists had hard lives. There was no meat, there were times when food was rationed. There was a song that went "When the day breaks, Poles get the straw and the Russians wheat."

Yet he concludes that things were, in fact, better before the war than during or after.

Ah. It was easier. We ate better more often... it was better. I was already married then, we had a wedding and lived together... otherwise it would have been hard for me to get by. It was large, but there was always work. I worked really hard, I tried everything.

I even spent five weeks under arrest because I sold my horse without paying the tax. My wife had to borrow money from a parish priest to pay this tax, and after five weeks I was set free. I was in jail in Pultusk. I got locked up on Christmas Day.

Leopold's grandson, Marek Stanowski, leads the way to the family plot in Chodkowo-Kuchny. Leopold's father is buried here.

Leopold and his wife Rozalia, also born in 1917.

The headstones from the town's Jewish cemetery,rescued from their desecration by the Nazis and turned into a monument.

This region of Poland, just north of the capital, Warsaw, was only barely, and technically, part of Russia at the time of Leopold's birth. Eastern Poland and Warsaw were absorbed into the Russian Empire at the time of the Second Partition, in 1793. Ruled as a semi-independent duchy, Poland, in fact, received a better deal (no serfdom, freer laws on assembly and representation) than did Russia proper – which led to a certain amount of resentment among those yearning for a parliament in St. Petersburg and an end to serfdom.

Poles meanwhile chafed against their status as a dominion, particularly in the latter half of the nineteenth century. The country was taken by German forces in the First World War and remained so up through the Russian Revolutions in 1917. It gained *de jure* independence from Russia in 1918, thanks to the Treaty of Versailles. But this was reaffirmed in fact when the young state defeated Russia in the 1919-1921 Polish-Soviet war that also played a bit part in staunching Lenin's European ambitions.

But independence was short-lived. The country was overrun by Nazi Germany on September 1, 1939, and by Soviet forces from the East on September 27 – the country's fate had been sealed the month before in the secret protocols of the Molotov-Ribbentrop Pact. The region where Leopold and his family lived was under German control.

When the war started I had just ended my apprenticeship as a butcher and I had been helping one out for a couple of months, and soon, the war came. We were retreating left and right. I am a butcher by trade, I make sausages... I fled, and then the war ended. I mean, the battles ended, the war was still going on. I worked, I catered weddings. I earned money through my trade.

I was seventeen when I started to work. I spent three years learning.

Two years into the war, Leopold met Rozalia. She too was born in 1917.

We went to school together, but she didn't like me then. Under the Germans, we had to go to Płoniawy for fingerprinting [for a photo ID]. My future wife was working for her brother at a neighboring meat shop. She came to ask me to slaughter a pig for her brother. So she joined us on our cart and rode home with us. I liked her so much that I thought: "That's one fine woman." So little by little, we fell in love. She is from Płoniawy, and I am from the village to the north, Bobino Wielkie.

But the reality of life in Poland during the war was harsh and complicated.

The Germans... It was a hard life. Not free. You weren't allowed to slaughter your own pig. If you got caught, you would be sent to a labor camp. You could not keep too many fowl. The Germans were always looking for grain for their army...

One Sunday in autumn people came to church wearing coats and fur, men and women, and the Germans took their clothes for the army in the East, where it was too cold for them. That's how they took clothes from people...

The Germans were bad to Poles. Regular soldiers, though, were mostly good people. Once, when we had Germans quartered in our village (and in our house, too), when I went to my plot to do some digging, a soldier came running up to me and then he carried my spade for me for half a mile, and when I was coming back he would do the same. When he got called up to go back to the front, he cried, and so did we. Privates, regular soldiers were very polite people. But the officers were bastards. They thought very little of Poles.

Did they know at the time that the Jews were being rounded up and what was happening to them, or did they only find out later?

We knew about the German camps and the Russian ones during the war, as everything was going on.

A look of deep anguish overcomes him, and he wipes his face with his hand. A long silence follows.

We knew about the German camps and the Russian ones during the war, as everything was going on.

Before the Second World War, the population of Maków-Mazowiecki, the small farming town that is the district center, was 7000. Just under half of the population, or about 3000 souls, were Jews, living in a ghetto on one side of town. After the Germans came barreling through on their machines of terror and murder, all of the Jews were rounded up and sent to camps. The town's large Jewish graveyard was ransacked and its gravestones were used to pave the sidewalks.

To pave the sidewalks.

Today, a bus station stands where the Jewish graveyard used to be. It is not clear what happened to all the interred remains, if the Germans dug them up and desecrated them, or if they were simply left in place (90 percent of the town was destroyed when Soviet forces retook this area).

But in the 1980s the town erected a monument made from headstones that had been saved from the sidewalks. Shaped like a pyramid, it overlooks the cracked and uneven payment of the bus station. A simple plaque reads, in Hebrew and Polish, "*Nasze slonce zgaslo nagle i ciemnosc w poludnie nastala*" (Our sun went out suddenly and the sun set in the middle of the day.)

With liberation came retributions and further privation.

I remember the Germans fleeing and Russians coming. They took the last cows. There was hunger during the Russian occupation. The occupations were hard, neither was a good time. Neither side treated us well. Now times are better...

After the war, every year was good. Sometimes worse, sometimes better, but, as a young man, I always got by. Even under arrest. I can't say it was great, but it wasn't that tragic, either...

Leopold shows his skill at playing a foot-pump accordion.

I have memories of occupation, of its beginning and end, and me going back to my normal life. I was just a butcher and nothing more. I worked weddings all around Poland...

I didn't have it too bad under the communists, or the Germans. I could always find work and was always in demand. Make some smoked meat, this, that.

Part of what helped make life easier for Leopold and his family was his election as village head after the war. He was selected through a village vote.

There was a gathering. "Who wants to be the head? You? Here you go." So I stayed that way for thirty-two years. I was busy with my own household, I was a butcher, and also the village head. Lots of trading but few gains.

Today, reflecting on his long life, he bemoans only his loss of mobility or ability.

If only I still had my good eyes and my hearing, my health, I would fly with the birds now. But the glaucoma ruined my eyes and I'm growing deaf. Should get a hearing aid, but then my vision is worse. I can only see that you are sitting in front of me, but I can't see what you look like. I'm deaf and blind. But that's just how it is. I still perform. When I'm in Maków, like I was in winter, and we put on a show there at the seniors club, people already know who I am and they say, "If the grandpa is performing, we shall come, but if he doesn't, then there's nothing to see here..."

I wouldn't live for another fifty years, but another fifteen would be nice. But these days, four months would be a miracle. My sight and hearing are not the same anymore, but sight is more important. Until last year, I rode a scooter. I still have it, it's in the garage. I'll leave it to my grandkids.

And after all that, Leopold offers a rather modest, if inaccurate, assessment of the century that has been his life.

My whole life was normal, really without extraordinary stuff.

MARFA STEPANOVNA KONECHNYKH

KRASNOYARSK

24 APRIL 1917

At least three times Marfa Konechnikh cheated death. Her daughter jokes that it was because her mother changed her birth name at an early age and, since on all her official documents she was named as Maria, Death simply couldn't find her. But likely it has more to do with Marfa's abundance of grit and determination. The first thing she says when her visitors arrive is this:

I don't want to die. Everything is gone, but we survived. Few of us survived. But I survived. I still want to live.

According to Marfa, on the day she was born her father held her in his arms and said to her mother:

"I will die, and I will take our daughter with me... Don't cry Tatyana Fyodorovna, you have six children, I will take our daughter with me." But to this day he has not taken me. That's what Mama said.

This may be family legend, because Marfa's father actually did die within 24 hours of Marfa's birth.

He went hunting squirrels. On the river, to the border he went. They caught a fish. And they ate the fish, and he got a sore throat and he died from his throat. Father did. That's what Mama said. I was still little and she told me that he... ate some kind of unhealthy fish. Big one. They said it was just lying there dead. They grabbed it, cooked it and ate it. And he died.

Restless and spry, Marfa moves around her apartment like a 70-year-old, worrying about whether this or that should be attended to, for example, if her guests have enough tea. She has small, narrow features and piercing blue eyes,

yet her limbs and fingers are long and slender, with no sign of arthritis or other serious ailments, other than the loss of sight in one eye.

Her parents were Old Believers, and Marfa was born in Arkhangelskoye village, Zabaikal Oblast, east of Lake Baikal. She had six sisters and a brother. After her father died, she would have just eight or nine years with her mother before becoming an orphan.

A bullet felled Mama. She was walking and some kids were sitting around, goofing off. And that goofing off killed her. My brother, who was 14, and two others were sitting in the corridor. She walked in from the street and arrived on the porch just in time to get hit by a bullet. Unlucky...

The boys had been playing with a hunting rifle that Marfa's brother had insisted their mother buy him, so he could hunt for food. It had been loaded with a bullet he intended to use on a she-bear, but the gun went off by accident and now the seven sisters and one brother were left without a mother.

My sister took me home. But she was no sister but a boorish woman. She needed to take all of Mama's property. There were two homes – she took them and sold them. Brother and sister were put out on the street, and I was taken to her home. I did not live with her, but was a slave... There were seven of us sisters and she was the only one like this. All of them were good, only she was like this. She had to have everything. Mama died and she took me from the kolkhoz... I washed the floors, did the laundry, watered and weeded the garden, all that stuff was mine to do. I was simply driven like a donkey. No time to eat and nothing to eat. How I survived, I don't know. I lived very badly in childhood. I didn't have a childhood. Girls came around, to invite me to go to school, and she says, "But who will work then? She is not going anywhere." My girlfriends all went, but I was not allowed...

The sister, Arina, had four daughters.

The daughters grew up and were given schooling, but I was not allowed. The four daughters were literate, but I remained a fool. [cries] My life was awful.

When MArfa was twelve, her sister dumped her at a kolkhoz in Buryatia, a region south and east of Lake Baikal. Her brother was taken into the army and she was completely alone.

I went to the chairman. He says, "And what can you do?" I says, "Whatever you order me to, I can do it. I can mow, I can harvest, I can plow." I did all that at my sister's. I was her worker. Only she didn't respect me.

By the 1940s, Marfa had become indispensable at the kolkhoz, teaching the younger workers how to work. She recalls how, when they tried to get her to join the army after the war broke out, her boss, the chairman, said,

"It would be better if I went into the army. I won't let her go." They took him and left me... He said, "If she goes, the kolkhoz will fall apart."

Marfa at the end of the 1940s or early 1950s and, below, Marfa today.

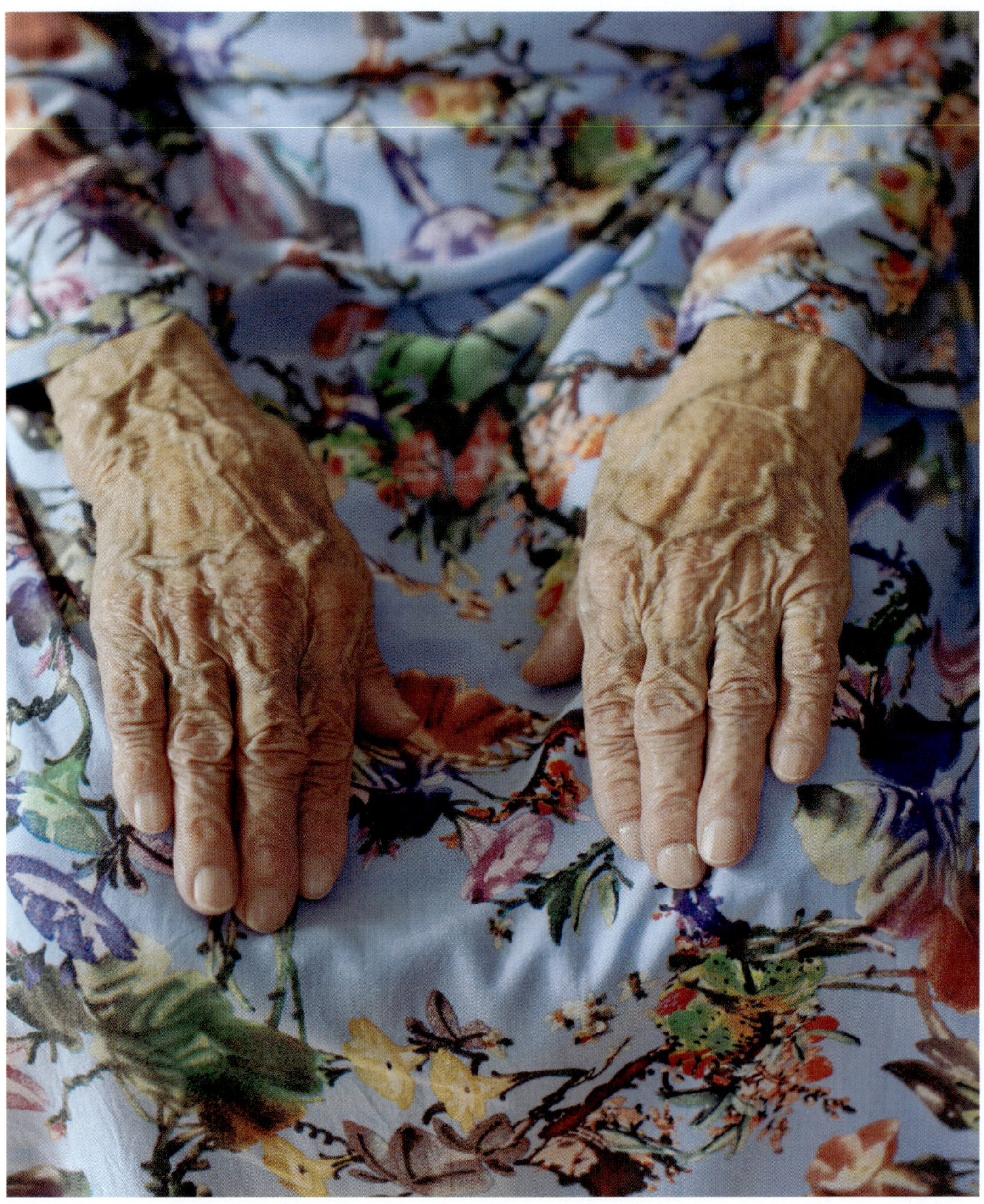

She spent the war working in the kolkhoz, and then in very physical labor felling timber and getting it to the river on horse-drawn vehicles.

It was difficult work. A lot of people drowned. If one fell into the river, one had to grab onto two logs and swim. They'd give me a slice of bread, it got wet, but I gobbled it up, whatever it was... What can you say? I am still alive.

When the war was won, Marfa recalls that there was no celebration, no day off...

Everyone was hungry. There was no one to give a day off to. There were no men, only women and children were left. We had no sort of holiday. We were just happy about the victory, but there was no day off. A holiday you gotta celebrate and observe, but who was there to do the celebrating? Children and old women... We were horribly hungry. But we survived. And we're even living now. Now there's something to eat and wear. But back then, there wasn't nothing. We spun hemp ourselves and wove it, and sewed shirts and skirts. That's what we wore. Put on your stiff clothing and set off. And it shuffles like a brush, that hemp stuff. But we survived.

After the war, Marfa worked as a senior baker, and early in the 1950s moved to the village of Ilka, in Buryatia. There she met Lavrenty Pavlovich (who didn't like his name, so insisted on being called Gennady*) and they had two children, Nikolai, born in 1953, and Tatyana, born in 1957.

It was actually Marfa's second marriage. The first one did not work out.

I left him. He was crap. Not a husband, but crap.

Marfa and Lavrenty got married in 1957.

What wedding? We drank some tea and that was it.

They bought a little plot of land and rebuilt the banya that stood on it into a home. They lived there for ten years and then moved to Krasnoyarsk because life was draining out of the kolkhoz. They were helped in making the move by two of the nieces that Marfa had helped raise while working for her sister Arina.

When they decided to travel, Marfa tried to buy tickets, but they wouldn't sell them one for the family dog, Valet, Marfa's daughter Tatyana recalls. "They decided that Papa would ride in the cargo car with Valet..." But then her brother Nikolai said he was going to ride with father and the dog as well, and then soon all four family members had decided to ride with Valet. Even so, the dog was also not allowed to ride in the cargo car, Tatyana says, "but that dog was smart. We would pull into a station and he would go hide in the corner and go quiet. He could not be seen or heard." But when they arrived in Krasnoyarsk, the sister Arina, who was now living with the two daughters, said they had to get rid of

* His name and patronymic, Lavrenty Pavlovich, was shared with Beria, Stalin's notorious Minister of Internal Affairs (and thus head of the NKVD).

Marfa with her husband, children, and relatives.

Marfa at work.

Valet: "We have one already, why would we need two dogs?" Tatyana recalls her saying. "So we gave the dog to some relatives who lived not far away. And we would frequently go and visit him."

Arina charged them rent for staying with them, but when the daughters found out, they insisted Arina return the money to Marfa's family, down to the last kopek.

Tatyana also offers another story, from back when her mother was working on the kolkhoz, before she was married. Apparently, Marfa was given a cow as a prize for hard work. And, since she had no children, she decided to take the cow to her sister (not Arina, but another one). And she walked the entire way with the cow – over a hundred kilometers – on foot, overnighting in the forest without a fire, for fear that she would be discovered and someone might kill her to get the cow.

To live, that is all. To live and be happy. Be happy with life, and to live.

All her life Marfa has been largely illiterate and to this day reads very poorly. It is a source of some shame and embarrassment for her. Yet she expresses great pride that, despite all that, she was always known as a particularly good and hard worker.

Everyone knows me by my work. Wherever I worked, I was always on the board of honor. I was first class. And my last job I worked in a garage... I was going home and the boss says, "Marfa Stepanovna, sit in the car."

And I says, "What for?"

"It will take you home."...

"And why me?"

"For your good work."

I cleaned the streets so well there, that there was not a bit of trash... I worked as a laundress, but I also cleaned up the street... He says, "We never had such a laundress. You used to come into our place and no matter where you stepped on the floor, it was dirty. But your floors shine. You are superb." They all loved me.

What does one need to eat to live to be 100?

Don't eat fatty foods. Just tea and a bit of bread. Some milk, sour cream. And meat is not really essential if you want to live. That's how you survive.

And what does she think, why are we here on earth?

To live, that is all. To live and be happy. Be happy with life, and to live. Whatever will be, will be. But still, be happy about life.

If the first time Marfa cheated death was surviving against the odds of orphanhood and living into maturity, the second time she cheated death was when she licked kidney cancer when she was about 50.

The third time was when she overcame pneumonia a few years later, well into her retirement. The doctor was sure that Marfa was dying and stopped by the family's house to ask, "Why have you not come by to pick up a death certificate?"

"What death certificate?" her daughter Tatyana replied. "Mama is cleaning the windows."

Then, 20 years ago, at 79, Marfa fell and broke her hip. The doctor said it would take a few months to heal, that for younger patients such a break usually heals in two months. But the ever-restless Marfa insisted that they make an X-ray of her just a month after the break. The doctor reported a phenomenal outcome: her bone had already healed, and quite strongly at that.

Marfa, her daughter Tatyana and son-in-law, Oleg, wave from the balcony of her thrid-floor apartment.

FYODOR LEONTIYEVICH SVISTUNOV

GORNY VILLAGE, KRASNODAR KRAI

25 APRIL 1917

Every word Fyodor Svistunov utters requires incredible effort. He squeezes each one out with a heavy sigh, as if it were his last. And then, noisily and convulsively, like a drowning man, he draws in a breath of air. He would love to speak more, but it is too tedious a task for his century-old lungs and vocal chords.

Fyodor smiles and gazes at his wife with hope and thankfulness. Yevdokia Stepanova has for many years now been his hands, feet, eyes, and lips. She is 11 years his junior and noticeably more active. Fyodor's hearing is decent enough, however, to allow him to silently participate in the conversation, nodding in agreement with what his wife says and offering an occasional word of assent.

Fyodor was born on April 25, 1917, in the village of Georgiyevka, in the Tuapse Okrug of the Chernomorsk (Black Sea) Gubernia. At that time, this part of Russia was still rather new. The Caucasian territories had only been tacked onto the empire half a century before the revolution. Most of the residents of Georgiyevka were Russian Cossacks or their descendants, who had transformed themselves into peasant farmers.

During the Civil War, the region changed hands several times. The mountains and forests along the shores of the Black Sea were alternately controlled by Reds, Whites, and Greens. The lattermost was a third, lesser-known, yet very serious force in the Civil War. Half-Anarchists, they fought "against all."

Yevdokia recalls how, during the time of revolutionary troubles, her husband miraculously gave Death the slip. Fyodor's father, Leonty, had gone off to fight for the Bolsheviks, and his mother Anna was left at home with four sons. The Greens took over their village and decided they would punish the

Fyodor and Yevdokia as newlyweds in 1948 (opposite page), and today (below).

local families of Reds, but that the reprisals on women and children should be meted out by others: namely by militant Caucasians who had suffered at the hands of Russians.

And they rounded up all the women and children in the village. And they led them to a large aul. And they said to them, "Shoot them." And these... what were they?..."*

Fyodor, who has been attentively following the conversation, slips in:

Cherkessians.

Yevdokia continues:

...Cherkessians. And they say, "No. If we shoot them, then the Reds will come and shoot us, and we will all end up dead. Better to let them live, and we will live alongside them." The moment passed, the coup ended, and they all returned to Georgiyevka with their children. The children lived, and everything turned out okay.

Fyodor's father returned from the Civil War, was renowned, yet was also a hard-drinking hunter. In fact, his fame as a hunter was so great that they wrote about him once in the papers. Fyodor was serving in the army in the Far East at that time, and they mailed him the article.

Young Fyodor had yet to meet his future wife. Her parents had moved to Georgiyevka in 1939, and she was too young for him to have paid any attention to her before he entered the army that year. Yet she well remembers the impressive funeral that Fyodor's famous father was given.

In the first year of the Second World War, Fyodor returned from the Far East to his home region of the Kuban. Yet it was not to rest, but to fight. Chance sent him to defend Novorossiysk, a huge port city about 150 kilometers from Georgiyevka. He served in the infantry, descended into the horrendous meat grinder of the front lines, was wounded multiple times and, during a retreat of Soviet forces, was taken prisoner.

During his imprisonment, Fyodor was operated on without anesthesia. The operation was successful in that he survived, but to this day he has mine shrapnel in his hand and spine.

Aftere he had recuperated, Fyodor was sent to a prisoner of war camp in Austria, where, along with other prisoners, he was put up "for sale." Austrian farmers would come to the camp, looking for workers. They would ask a single question: "You a kolkhoznik?" If you answered "yes," they would gladly take you. But all the over-educated and supra-literate prisoners were left behind in the camp.

* A Caucasian village.

Fyodor, Yevdokia and their two eldest sons in the 1950s.

Fyodor's son gives him a close shave for the camera. Below, a domestic still life.

To be fair, many German and Austrian burghers dealt decently with their Ostarbeiters – the slave labor force captured from the war in the East. But Fyodor was not so lucky: his boss was very strict and would beat him with a stick for the slightest infraction.

When, in 1945, Soviet troops began to occupy Austria, the fascists retreated along with the loyalist burghers, who also took their slave laborers. During the panicked evacuation, Fyodor and six comrades hid in an attic, inside wine barrels. They only emerged when Russian soldiers arrived on the farm.

An unenviable fate awaited Fyodor. The motherland did not look kindly on Soviet soldiers who had been taken prisoner. Upon their release from POW camps, hundreds of thousands of Soviet prisoners were immediately shipped to labor camps in their homeland, because they were unable to prove that they had been captured against their will. But Fyodor passed his interrogation with the secret police: he merely had to show his wounds.

Yet he was still not allowed to return home, and was sent to the Far East to finish his military service. There the war with Japan was winding down. And so it was only in 1946 that Fyodor finally saw his mother again.

Yevdokia tells how once, after the war, she and some girlfriends were divining who their future husbands might be. And she had a dream of someone in an overcoat. And that is exactly how she first saw Fyodor, upon his return to Georgiyevka:

Others returned from the front with large quantities of stolen goods. But he was poor: all he had was his overcoat and a towel.

After the war, many girls were alone: young and unmarried. He offended none and called on everyone. We met and he stopped visiting others.

Others returned from the front with large quantities of stolen goods. All he had was his overcoat and a towel.

Fyodor does not object to his wife's openness, only offering a sidelong glance.

The couple had children one after another: five boys in all, but two died in infancy. In 1953 the family moved a bit higher into the mountains, to the tiny village of Gornoye, hidden behind thickets of forest. The Svistunovs for the most part lived off the forest. They labored with fruit harvested from the wild: pears and cherries, chestnuts and acorns. Yevdokia was hired at an industrial fruit drying operation, and spent her days shoveling fruit. Fyodor worked as a carter at a factory that produced chicory as a coffee substitute.

And together they made wooden supports for grape vines out of tree trunks. The Kuban had a fair number of winemakers and the Svistunov's output was in high demand.

We'd cut down the trees that were about two meters high, then cut them into four pieces of this sort of thickness... This entire area near our house was full of them. We'd pile them up into heaps as best we could, and then a truck would come and we'd load up the piles.

The couple became accustomed to working together, helping and safeguarding one another. And they were so friendly with one another that their neighbors were always surprised: a coarse word never wafted over from their yard.

But of course, life was not all work.

We went to the movies. Went to the sea. When he was working, we drove to the sea every weekend. We swam. To the buoys, he and I swam. Even to the buoys we swam. We'd rest there and then swim back. And when he went on his pension, there was no more time for that. We stopped driving to the sea. Always home, home. That's how it is. Always home, home.

From their harvesting of the forest's wealth, the Svistunovs earned enough for a modest home. And to this day the couple lives in the tiny, two-room hut, with its white walls and low ceilings.

Generally, everything was good. And I never swore at grampa, and he never cursed me for anything either. That's how we lived. He always called me, "Dusya-Dusya-Dusya." And after children, there were grandchildren, and we became grandpa and grandma.

Yevdokia turns to her husband, who is sitting alongside her.

You see there, grampa, I did all your speaking for you: both about how you love me, and how you swore at me. Tell me, did you ever once swear?

Fyodor answers her with an honest and tender gaze:

No, I don't remember once.

His wife laughs and claps him on the shoulder. In reply, his lips part in a weak smile.

Well, that's all that he told me before his memory completely left him. But I've already forgotten plenty. What the future holds, how much longer we will live, I don't know. Or how many days or nights, or months or years, God has left for us. But grampa and I have lived them together, thank God. May everyone live as well as we have.

"We've still plenty to live," Fyodor jokes, surprising everyone with his hard-won interjection, sly sparks illuminating his deep blue eyes.

Outside the Svistunov home.

TAMARA IVANOVNA SUDAKOVA

MINDERLA VILLAGE, KRASNOYARSK KRAI

29 APRIL 1917

About an hour's drive from downtown Krasnoyarsk, partway down a dirt road in the village of Minderla (population 2000; chief industry: turkey farm), there is a modest duplex home. Half of it is well cared for: painted bright shades of blue and yellow, with new fiberglass windows and a well-tended yard. The other half is run-down, unpainted, and untended.

A tall, well-built man with stark, Scandinavian features strides out from behind the fence on the brightly painted side, introduces himself as Vladimir, and quickly adds that he has driven here from a neighboring town, and thus he won't be able to imbibe.

"Imbibe?" reply the arriving journalists. "But we came here to work!" What is more, said journalists have forgotten to pick up a gift "for the table," so it would be very uncomfortable to sit down for a meal.

But Vladimir and family will have none of it. "We are Russians, we can't help ourselves," he laughs, pointing as the group enters the home to a long table stacked with fresh vegetables, potatoes, chicken, mushrooms, and, of course, vodka.

Tamara Sudakova, like her son Vladimir, has an elongated, distinguished northern visage. The 100-year-old skin below her eyes sags, giving her the appearance of someone who is very sad, yet she is nothing of the sort. Instead, she is loquacious, with a superb and detailed memory, has a winning sense of humor, and has composed hundreds of poems, none of them written down. She is not shy about reciting them at opportune moments.

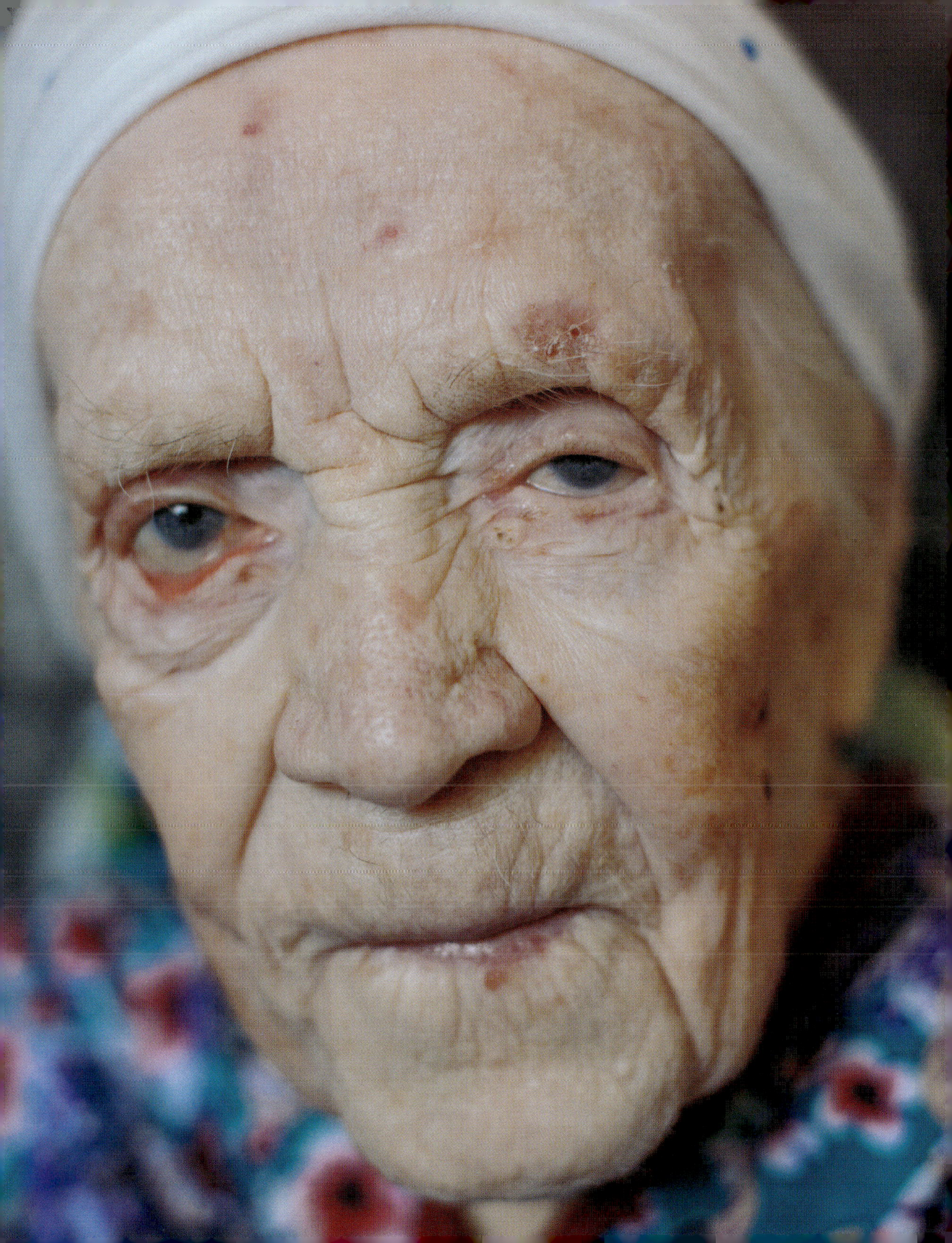

A single question elicits a 15-minute story, grippingly told and filled with astounding detail. On some topics, she laughs repeatedly between thoughts, as if to underscore the irony of something she endured. And she repeatedly calls her visitors "comrades," because that is the form of address she used all her life, and it works just fine.

Tamara was born in the village of Volkova, 300 kilometers east of Petrograd,* just two months after the start of the February Revolution, and hers was a family of hard-working, modestly successful farmers.

They were peasant stock. Father had three desyatins† of land that he had to cultivate during the summer. It was such a difficult period to work and earn one's bread. First, you had to keep animals, in order that they produced manure, and that had to be taken out to the fields... My father sat me on top of a horse at nine and had me harrow‡ the fields. That was the start of my working life. But before that they reaped the fields with a sickle and sang. I really wanted to learn to reap and sing. So I stole Mama's sickle on the sly. And I went – I was eight then – into the fields. I, of course, knew where the rye was... And I started singing:

Masha once reaped a strip of land, golden sheaves she wove.
But she dared not say a thing, for here the revolution had taken hold.

I have no idea where I learned that chastushka. But Mama discovered me, took away the sickle and said... well, in the end, I learned anyway to tie sheaves, I mean, to reap... There was a lot of work, in order to make things better. Because there, in that region, wheat didn't grow. Only rye, barley, and oats... And there was hay – over 12 kilometers away. Mama walked there to and from, but Papa just lived there while they were mowing. We had a cow at home and it had to be milked and so on. So that's how they lived. It was horrible; my parents did not see anything good.

---

* Founded by Peter I in 1703 and named St. Petersburg, the city was the capital of the Russian empire from 1713-1728 and 1732-1918. It was renamed Petrograd in 1914 because Russia was at war with the Kaiser and Petersburg sounded too German. The city was renamed Leningrad in 1924, to honor the first Soviet leader (who was actually born Ulyanov, and who had moved the capital to Moscow in 1918). In 1991, the city's original name, St. Petersburg, was restored through a popular referendum.

† A *desyatina* was literally a "tenth," because originally it was a square plot of land that was one-tenth of a *verst* (about a kilometer) on each side, resulting in 2500 square *sazhens*. It is roughly equivalent to 2.7 acres, so the family farm was just over 7 acres. The use of the term *desyatina* was outlawed in the USSR in 1927, about the time Tamara was first harrowing the fields. In 1918 Russia adopted the metric system.

‡ Harrowing involves dragging a sharp-tooted or disked implement over the fields in order to level the land, to break up clods and uproot weeds.

Above, Tamara Sudakova and her family. She is seated, far right, and her husband Nikolai is standing, far left. Below, the house taken from her family in Leningrad Oblast.

Indeed, the good times were few and far between.

Ilya's Day, on the second, was the patron saint's holiday in our village. For that holiday they even came back from the haying. But no one made moonshine, they just brewed beer... There were no fights, no scandals. Just accordion and music. They'd walk around the village, singing. People came to visit, drink tea, then went on to the next house. It was a peaceful time... I was so brave, I am surprised myself how I feared nothing back then. Once they sent me 10 or 20 kilometers on foot to get honey from an acquaintance...*

That was my life. No fruit passed our lips. [laughs] For us, fruit was rutabaga, steamed and fried. Turnips, carrots, that's it. It's how we lived. Maybe it made us stronger... But everyone worked, everyone. It made us... We were more independent...

And for that, they would pay.

Grampa, Papa's father, was a trader... Someone brought him goods to our village and he sold them... kerosene... herring... sugar, salt, a bit of manufactured goods... tobacco...

But, then in the 1930s the dekulakization started. They started taking homes away from the peasants who were better off, to exile them hither and yon. Our house was fancied as a hospital. And so they drove us out of our home... It was summer and we really didn't expect it. My sister and I, we were sitting and playing, and Papa had gone off somewhere... A policeman comes and says, "Hey, you, march outta here!" I was so afraid that I froze. Then he says, "I said, get out of here!" My sister and I fled, crying, and he put a lock on the house and that was it. We saw momma coming out of the summer kitchen with my little brother, and he's crying too, and only then did we understand they were kicking us out of our home...

The family wintered over in a dilapidated, abandoned hut adjoining an old church. Neighbors helped them out, and they were able to sneak back to their garden and dig up vegetables buried there.

I remember when we left it was on sleds. They took us to Babayevo Station. Someone came over and said, "Leave Tamara with us, we will take her to Leningrad." Mama refused, crying, "At least we will all die together..." They shipped us out in train cars... [treated us] worse than cattle. Worse. Freight cars that were very dirty. They shipped us to Mogocha Station. Of course, we traveled for a long time, so they fed us some swill or other. Enough to keep us from going hungry, but not enough so that we would be filled.

---

* August 2 (July 20, Old Style), celebrated in honor of St. Elijah, one of Russia's most venerated saints. In the Slavic folk tradition, Elijah was the master of thunder, heavenly fire, and rain, the patron of the harvest and fertility. His name day was one of the major pre-revolutionary holidays.

When they arrived at Mogocha,* a town 700 kilometers east of Chita, the family was split up. Her father was sent to work in the mines, and the children and their mother were sent to live in barracks. Tamara was then 14, and she and three other girls were put to work driving horse carts filled with dung, and then minding chicken coops, where they had to keep the inside temperature at 38° Celsius (100° Fahrenheit), carefully turning over eggs, occasionally slipping outside into the bitter cold, just to breathe fresh, cool air.

In the spring, Tamara's mother fell sick and the children were living alone in a barracks when the river Mogocha flooded. Many fled the rising waters in time, but for some reason the children were left behind, and so they climbed up onto the top bunks, hoping the waters would recede.

The door was torn off the barracks, and the water came rushing in. Then a second door was torn off and the water rushed through like a river. Do you understand? It was horrifying. The noise, the river rushing right by, and we were on the top bunks – me, my sister, and my two-year-old brother. Someone else was sitting in the corner. An old man and an old woman. Everyone else had fled... No one else was there. Then we looked up and saw that – can you imagine – a boat was floating right up to our bunk. Yes, a boat floated up, and they say, "Get in." We got into the boat and as we start to leave the barracks in the boat, they say to us, "Duck your heads." And we had only just ducked, only just gotten out of the barracks, floated away a bit, when behind us floated the very boards that we had been sitting on. A few moments more and we would have drowned there. That's the sort of life we had.

A few moments more and we would have drowned there.

Their father finally returned in the fall.

We met Papa with tears of joy because he had come back alive. But many cried because theirs had died in the mines. And then they took us back here, to Krasnoyarsk... and we were already more free. They offered to send us back to our home region. But what was there for us back there, when they had taken everything from us?...

When I arrived [in Krasnoyarsk], I had only had four years of schooling, because our village had only had a primary school... And here I started studying in an evening school. I started working.

First, they put her to work in a cafeteria for "special resettlers" [a euphemism used for exiled kulaks – see note, page 92], helping the cook, setting tables, and washing dishes.

I was so satisfied that I had work. I worked two days... and some man and woman arrived. "What are you doing here, little girl?" And I replied so proudly, "I am working.

---

* Mogocha, located less than 100 kilometers from the border with China, was the center of a gold mining industry and, in the post-War period, would become an administrative center for the region's labor camps.

Scenes from Tamara's home in Minderla.

I am working." He quickly goes into the kitchen, and I hear at first a quiet discussion and then it gets much louder. The cook she comes out, crying. The man says, "Ok, you, go home." Yes, me. "You are too young to be working here," he says. I was able to work with horses, but here I could not work with dishes.

There followed grueling work as a foot messenger for a government gold mining concern, where she would often walk from one end of the city to the other, carrying messages between offices in the pre-telephone era. She remembers walking in her faux leather boots, and when she took them off upon arriving, her *portyanki* [foot wraps] froze to the inside of her boots. She would then walk around the office, "warming up my feet while they sorted out the documents before sending me off again."

The following summer her father was summoned to help build the city's Dinamo Stadium, and the family moved into barracks near the site, working at various construction jobs and taking in laundry.

And then the war began.

As it turned out, just before that I had finished night school and entered the teachers' training school. I studied there for two years and then the war came... I remember how that evening, the senior students – not my class – had a dance. We goofed off and had fun all night... we even ran down the mountain – there was a mountain here where everyone would gather to relax. We arrived home and, at four in the morning, war was declared. It didn't really affect us so much because the Finnish war had been so quick – it began and ended... But I remember how papa stood there and said, "Bad, children, bad. This war will be horrible, horrible." And it lasted four years...

And Tamara pauses and recites a poem by Konstantin Simonov.

On that longest day of the year,
With its cloudless skies,
We were given a common misfortune
All of us, for four long years.
It left such a mark on us,
And crushed us so,
That twenty, thirty years on,
We, the living, don't believe we are so.

Truly, may no one have to live through what we did. Even today I remember many poems.

She recites another:*

Tender children of war,
Such misfortune you have survived,
Life would have been so different,
If your father had lived.
The bitter pill of orphanhood
You received so young,
And, in spite of your age
You began work young.
On the fields and in the factories
Replacing your fallen fathers,
Whom you bid farewell to as children,
And immediately became adults.

During the war, in 1942, Tamara began teaching in a kolkhoz school in Taloye, where she led classes for the next 30 years, throwing herself into the lives and learning of her charges.

I loved the children, and they all respected me. I never had any fights, none. The kids were very obedient. And they did all sorts of horrible work. In the village, in Taloye, women made bricks by hand. And then, when the bricks were ready, they were taken to a so-called kiln, but it was really just a pit. How it was made, I don't know, but the fact was that one had to walk a long way down... and when they were all baked and dried, they would send the fourth graders to carry them back up. I had the fourth grade one year. It was so scary. I went, thinking, "Please just let them all come back alive. Children get tired..." And when I led them back, I was so happy that they were all alive and not injured. It was such difficult work for children.

And potatoes? Back then in the fall, they gave our school 12, no not 12, 14 hectares to dig up by hand. The entire school went. The higher classes were off somewhere in the fields, and we, the poor ones, were with the first graders, gathering. One time, we women said, "Maybe we shouldn't take them, the first graders."

"No, dear ones, bring them. We know that you will keep a close eye on them."

The first-graders filled the buckets with the potatoes they dug up, and the older students carried them off and emptied them into big piles.

Classes started in the school at eight. We would shorten the breaks, only allowing the kids out to go to the bathroom. We would have classes, then the kids would run

* This is one she wrote.

home, quickly change, and then we would go into the fields to dig potatoes. We would dig until dusk, then take them home, where the poor things still had to do homework. And there was no electricity, so they worked by kerosene lamps.

It was in Taloye, after the war, that Tamara met her husband, Nikolai.

He was a happy person, Kolya. They were from Baikal. My husband's father was a veterinarian. A veterinarian, they say, who was anointed of God. He was strict but just... When they lived in Taloye they would come by to sit and talk. He served in the Far East. Then he went to America to get some ships... Once, during the war, he was sent from the East to the West on some secret mission. He [Nikolai] was on a train near Leningrad and it was bombed. He was injured in the leg, rested and healed a bit, then went back to his unit. He went here and there... They hid their wounds back then. They had decided they wanted to go the virgin lands. But if you said that you were wounded, they might not take you. Then they got as far as Krasnoyarsk and jumped off. There was, after all, lots of work here. And they stayed.

Nikolai was one of the lucky ones. Taloye sent 272 people to the front in World War Two; of them, 200 were killed.

Tamara's husband died in 1999, and Tamara moved to Minderla to live with her daughter Nina (born in 1949) and to be near her son Vladimir (born in 1950). And she is very clear about the benefits this has brought her.

The most important medicine, the best support, is when you have good, caring children. And in this respect, comrades, I am very happy, very. I have such caring children that some people even envy me... May you be healthy and may everyone have children like I have.

The most important medicine, the best support, is when you have good, caring children.

And when asked how one gets such caring, helpful children, Tamara answers with unbridled honesty.

I have no idea. I never saw them, comrades, because I [laughs] was so very busy: deputy of the village council, regional people's assessor; member of the women's council; member of the audit commission for stores. I never saw them. And on top of that, we had a certain type of school director.

Which leads her into a story about how, when she was due to give birth to Vladimir, the director was going off on a business trip and forbade her from taking any time off, else she would have no job when he returned.

And we, fools that we were, all believed him. Well, he left. And I almost gave birth in the school. A dog scared me. I was leaving school on a Saturday, and some strange dog ran at me. Maybe it was mistaken... But I gave birth to a poor boy, all blue... And then [the director] come back the next morning and summoned me to the school... He says [to another teacher],

"What, Sudakova not here?"

And she says, "She's not coming."

"What do you mean not coming?"

"Because she gave birth to a boy."

"How did she do that?"...

"The same way all women give birth."

"Well, let her rest then."

So she was given the then customary 21 days off work.

Today, Tamara's daily "regimen" is far more relaxed. She gets up at eight and spends much of her day weaving circular "carpets" from plastic bags that her family purchase at the local grocery store. She gifts them to friends and acquaintances, and her "*kruzhki*" (literally "little circles," because of their round shape), have now landed on floors well beyond Russia's borders.

To what does Tamara Ivanovna attribute her long life?

I think it is because I started work early. My organism sort of got stronger. I helped people who were doing good things. I was able to help. Then, I didn't have any harmful habits. My entire life, whether you believe it or not, I have only had a drink twice. Once, when I was 22, when seeing a neighbor off to the army... and then once when I was a teacher, in Taloye...

This leads her to recite yet another poem:

Beneath my window
There's a new arbor.
My husband's hooked up
With our new neighbor.
But she doesn't know
That the man's a drunk.
And now I worry
He might just come back.

And does she wonder, how her life might have turned out differently, had the revolution not happened?

Oh, I don't know anything about politics. How would life have turned out? We would have lived in Volkova and that's it. Perhaps it was all very difficult, what I have lived through... but if I had stayed in Volkova I would have just had four years of schooling. Yet here I was educated as a person. I've received all sorts of appreciation. And awards from Moscow. I lived for the children. Now they care for me in everything, as if taking care of a small child.

One of Tamara's "kruzhki" ("circle") rugs, which she weaves from plastic bags.

ALEXANDRA VASILYEVNA PILYASOVA

KHIMKI, MOSCOW OBLAST

20 MAY 1917

Alexandra Pilyasova is dressed simply but elegantly in a blue and purple dress, her head covered in a white and blue headscarf tied under the chin that does not want to stay put. She speaks in a slow, deliberate cadence often filled with long pauses. Her words and diction are clear, her voice is soft and round.

This spring, after her son died, Alexandra moved from Bashkiria to live with her daughter Tatyana in Khimki, just outside Moscow. The two share a roomy, tastefully-decorated apartment on a well-greened suburban street with two cats that Alexandra brought with her from Tirlyan. One of them is due to give birth any day.

I was born in the village of Tirlyan. And I studied there through the eighth grade. My father was in the revolution... he was the youngest brother, born in '81, and they took him into the army. He served seven years in the tsarist army. Then he returned and got married. My mother, she was a beauty.

Mama told me about how, after their church wedding, it was winter, and as they rode in the troika together, the couple threw bottles of beer to people they passed. As a present. And candy too. So that people would marvel at them, to show that they were not simple, not poor. He had served in the military, after all.

Father was a peasant, he worked the land. He had horses, cattle. When he married my mother, her father was doing a bit of trading, buying a bit then taking it somewhere to sell. Mama's dad said to my father: "Why are you keeping the horses? They should earn their feed." So my father hired two people to haul ore. And they took the ore to Magnitogorsk to sell.

Mama told me how Father served in the army. They gave him a watch and a sable for honest service. He was handsome, Father was. He had a beard, or rather mustaches. They would freeze in the winter. He would have to clean them because I was waiting to kiss him. Whenever my children go somewhere, they always kiss me. They should never go anywhere without saying goodbye. And I taught them to kiss. And at the table they always say "thank you" before getting up, thank God. They always said that.

At times, Alexandra's mind plays tricks on her, mixing up her own memories with stories her mother told her long ago about her own childhood and marriage to Alexandra's father. But then she retrieves a memory of how her father, after serving seven years in the tsarist army with distinction, fighting against the Japanese and Germans, later refused to fight for the Reds in the Civil War. "I'm done with fighting," he said.

My family were rural people, they all had good character. Yet in Tirlyan they still de-kulakized them for nothing. They were jealous that Mama and Father educated their children. One finished forestry school, another the technical school, and the third the Soviet party school. They were all party members. But then they all got kicked out of the party. My brother came back from a meeting and said to the family: "Leave, you are part of the de-kulakization."

But how can you leave your home? We did not leave until they forced us to. But leave we did. Father went to Agapovka, that's beyond Magnitogorsk. There he got work in a vegetable store. Apples, fruits – that's where he worked. Mother went to be with him later.

I stayed with my aunt, to be in school. Her husband worked in the factory. They kept them there because they needed them. They were not touched.

People were just jealous because my parents sent their kids to school. Our parents did everything to get us educated.

They drove us out of our home. They didn't know what article to charge us under, because we did not have a household of any size. Sure, a horse and a cow. But they still marked us up as enemies. In reality, we had nothing.

My earliest memory is of the kids in school. The girls felt sorry for me, but the guys said, "she's the daughter of a kulak." That was embarrassing. What sort of kulaks? We had a cow and a horse.*

---

* Kulaks: well-to-do peasants with hired laborers. By the late 1920s, when Collectivization of agriculture was underway, kulaks were made into scapegoats. In January 1930, the Soviet government issued a decree on "Liquidating the Kulaks as a Class," which many feel was a major contributing factor in the famine of 1932-33. Estimates of how many kulaks were exiled and/or executed vary widely. Soviet statistics say just under two million were exiled and 700,000 killed. Aleksandr Solzhenitsyn and Robert Conquest both estimated more than 6 million killed.

Alexandra, right, with her brother and a younger relative.

Alexandra's father served seven years in the tsar's army.

The family survived dekulakization but was split up. One brother moved to Mariupol, Ukraine, where he eventually married a local. Her younger brother Ivan, Alexandra recalls, choking up, tears filling her eyes at the 70-year-old memory, went to the front.

He went to wash off the label [of kulak] they had pinned on us. Still, we all tried to convince him not to go. His wife was with child. He said, "No, I am going to wash off the guilt." He had also studied at the party school.

And he was injured.

He would tell us he was saved by a dog. It got him to a medical station. He had been shot in the stomach. And he told me: "All my guts were hanging out. And what would a dog do?" He told everyone, "I pushed them back in by myself." And then he lost consciousness.

And that's how he came back to me, injured. Things were difficult. I wanted to feed him something. [cries] But there was nothing. We had just a little goat, so I slaughtered it and fed him. We lived through many difficulties. But he got better, and he got his old job back at the railroad. He suffered in vain.

I went to work at the factory when I was 20. It was difficult. After your shift all you wanted to do was sleep. My brother found me an apartment with very good people.

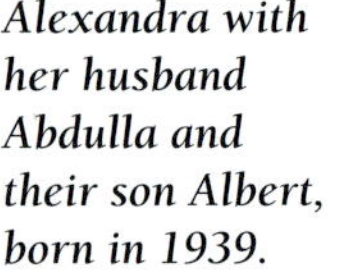

Alexandra with her husband Abdulla and their son Albert, born in 1939.

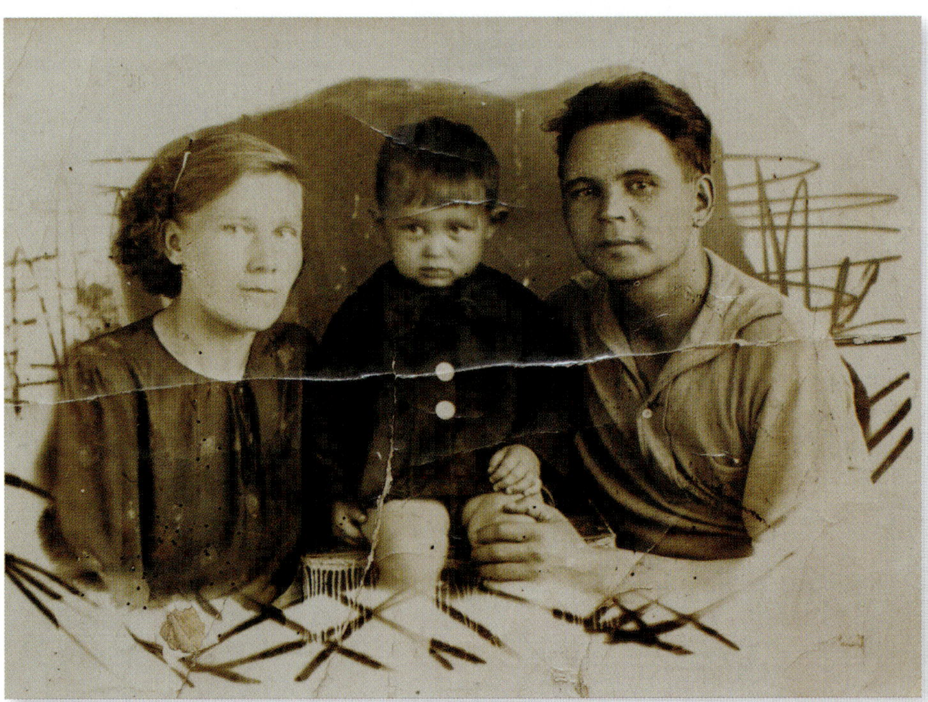

They also felt sorry for me. The husband had fallen into the works at the factory and a wire went straight through his foot. That's what work was like. But he got better and became a controller. They tried to help me. Got me a bit of milk. And I helped them. I went and dug potatoes with them. They had taken me in after all.

When I finished school, I got married. My older brother got me a job. He worked in the forge as a norm-setter. He got me a job as someone who weighed the items going into the furnace. I weighed things so that it was correct. They didn't weigh the coal, but the lime had to be exact... The workers were covered in dust. Well, that's just how I worked.

Then I got married. Everyone was afraid of me, because my father was de-kulakized, for no reason of course. But my husband was not afraid of me. He had graduated from a technical institute, and he was Tatar, not Russian.

Alexandra and Tatyana remember Abdulla (everyone called him Ivan), their husband and father, respectively, as a dedicated, highly talented engineer. Alexandra says Abdulla fell in love with her at first sight, "but I took a bit of time to come around," she laughs. Because Abdulla was so capable and so needed at the factory, the authorities were inclined to forget about her family's kulak past.

And I didn't rush to remind anyone.

We asked for a house. Previously, some homes like ours had been confiscated. But they gave me a private home, and my husband and I moved there. It had two rooms. We bought a cow. The factory gave us a pig so that we would work and have enough to eat. My husband was from Ufa, so he, of course, could not mow, but I was from Tirlyan, so I knew how. I taught him to mow hay. We walked on foot to mow hay then brought it home, working all day long. There was a lot of work.

The factory gave us a pig so that we would work and have enough to eat.

During the war, an acquaintance gave us a bit of land. We planted wheat there, then we harvested it ourselves, brought it home and milled the flour in the yard. That's how we worked.

When the war broke out, we were on vacation in Ufa, and then we came back home. I was not working at that time; I had a little boy, Albert. But when the war started, I had to put him in a kindergarten. They were asking me to come to work. I was made a controller. There were stores and they gave out ration coupons. We had to verify all the coupons. We carefully checked to make sure there was no funny business with produce. I worked at that for seven years, as a controller, giving out produce in stores in exchange for coupons.

My husband worked in the factory the whole war, in the blast furnaces, in the forges where they produced steel plates [for tanks].

After the war, after they stopped the ration coupons, a store asked me to come and work as a simple worker. I worked as a salesgirl.

When we had that rationing system, they awarded me a Stalin medal. I got a Stalin medal for good work. I got five more medals, for honest labor.

One of the most difficult realities of living to be 100 is that one has a good chance of outliving one's children. Earlier this year, Alexandra's son died after a long illness. Each time it comes up in her memory, she becomes inconsolable.

My son waited for me. He was living in Magnitka, and I was in Beloretsk. My daughter showed up: "Mama, he's in a bad way, we have to go." I went immediately, and I got there just before he died. He gave me his hand [cries]. I took his hand and he died.

We buried him there, in Magnitogorsk. He had built a home there. He worked and he helped me. My daughter had long been asking me to move to Moscow, but I could not leave my son behind. After he was buried, I finally agreed. He did not leave me, and so I could not leave him.

That's how it is with me, I left everything, even my house. I put it up for sale, but it still doesn't sell – it's the crisis. I just left everything. My grandson and great-grandson are still there.

I am with my daughter now, of course, and I will survive.

Change.

70 years and more I lived in my own home. But my path there is done now, and I will get accustomed to living with my daughter. My daughter, of course, looks after me.

And I brought my cats. I could not just leave them. I feel sorry for them. We took them to the doctor, got them all their shots, and put them on the plane with me.

Each cat's ticket cost 4000 rubles ($70), plus a passport costing another 500 rubles each. And there was to be no discount airfare for the fact that Alexandra was 100.

"Right!" says daughter Tatyana. "Discounts for 100-year-olds are not real, they are only something they write about."

Later, after a break for tea and pastries, talk turns to music and Alexandra recalls a poignant memory from her childhood.

When I was younger, I played the guitar. And I had a mandolin and a balalaika. I insisted that my parents buy me a guitar. But Mama said, "I am saving money, we will need it for your dowry after all." And I said, "I don't need anything. I need a guitar." And I performed on stage in school, and I sang.

I stopped playing the guitar when the grief became too great. I buried all my brothers. My daughter died. And now my son.

Yes, I have survived plenty. I have buried everyone.

"I have survived plenty. I have buried everyone."

ALEXANDRA NIKOLAYEVNA ANTONOVA
ST. PETERSBURG
7 JUNE 1917

Alexandra Antonova has not left her apartment for two years.

The outside world is somewhere on the other side of her plywood door – a door that does not fit very snugly in its jamb. Within the apartment, the clanking and creaking of the building's old elevator are distinctly audible, as is the relentless roar of planes landing and taking off from nearby Pulkovo Airport, one of Russia's largest international airfields.

Yet for a person who has lived for two years entirely between four walls, Alexandra is surprisingly active and upbeat.

If she so wishes, the world is at her feet. Wrapping herself in an elegant overcoat, she steps out onto her little balcony and, from her ninth-floor perch, surveys her surroundings. In her elegant fingers she grasps a set of miniature opera glasses and aims them at the endless rows of concrete panel high rises, or at the boundless grey skies above Petersburg.

If she desires, all of the wisdom of humankind is in the palms of her hands. On the shelves of a large, glass-fronted bookcase are 200 volumes of a library built years ago through subscription. Russian and foreign classics in fine Soviet editions are at her fingertips. And the favorites she returns to time and time again? Goldsworthy and Yesenin.

Alexandra carries herself calmly and with assurance, in complete control of her body. In order not to lose her vigor of mind or spirit, she exercises daily, taking 500 steps in a circular route around her apartment. The one-room apartment is not large, so this requires many circles. An additional measure: wiggling her toes, so that the blood does not pool in her feet.

She has the grace of an elderly queen and the buoyancy of a former ballerina. She has thin, soft skin and attentive eyes that retain their attractive azure luster. A hairdresser visited her a few days ago, and her thick, milky-white hair is tightly-curled, albeit lying on her head with a slight carelessness. A small necklace dangling a single pearl fills out her appearance as a true Petersburgian.

Truth be told, Alexandra is but a first-generation denizen of this northern city. She was born on June 7, 1917, in the village of Strugi-Belaya, Petrograd Gubernia, about 200 kilometers west of the capital. It is a poor region with soil that is poorer still, a risky place to own land. But Strugi was not merely a peasant village. It was also an important railway station, built in the middle of the nineteenth century and uniting the capital of the Russian empire with Warsaw.

Alexandra is a tireless storyteller with a superb memory. She recalls her small home village well.

It was a junction station with a steam depot, with a water tower to refill the steam engines. After the railway was built, people of lots of nationalities [who built the railway] settled in our town. We had Estonians, Latvians, Germans, Poles... we even had a Chinese man. How he ended up there, I have no idea. But Strugi was very beautiful. Everywhere was awash in green, in gardens. The people were so well-educated. If you came in from St. Petersburg, on the left side there was a shooting range, built on the orders of Nicholas II, which military units would frequent. And so we had lots of military there.

After the revolution, Strugi-Belaya was in territory occupied by opponents of the Bolsheviks – White Army units. But within a few months the Whites were forced out by the Red Army, pushed toward the South. And the town was renamed Strugi Krasnye ("Red Strugi"). Alexandra's father imprudently remarked on this several times, saying that "Our village changes its color depending on who is in charge on any given day."

Alexandra's father, Nikolai, became one of the most important persons in her life. He took the place of her mother and ably created a happy childhood for his children, despite the fact that the country was passing through a very complicated, hungry, and scary time.

I was not even a year old when my mother died. She had two older daughters, Maria and Olga, who had already finished at the gymnasium.[*] *But then they got sick with typhus and died. And Mama died of grief.*

But our Papa was very good. He had wives, but I don't recall calling anyone Mama. No one cared for us or protected us. I don't remember a female hand. Basically, Papa

---

* A special secondary school that prepares students for higher education.

Воинское бесплатное

Куда гор. Чебоксары, Чув. АССР п/я №12. ул. Чкалова д. №1, кв. 3

Кому Антоновой Александре Николаевне

Адрес отправителя ПОЛЕВАЯ ПОЧТА

Ленинград, 167. п/я №

(указать № полевой почты)

партбюро Васильев.

(фамилия, имя и отчество)

Привет с фронта!

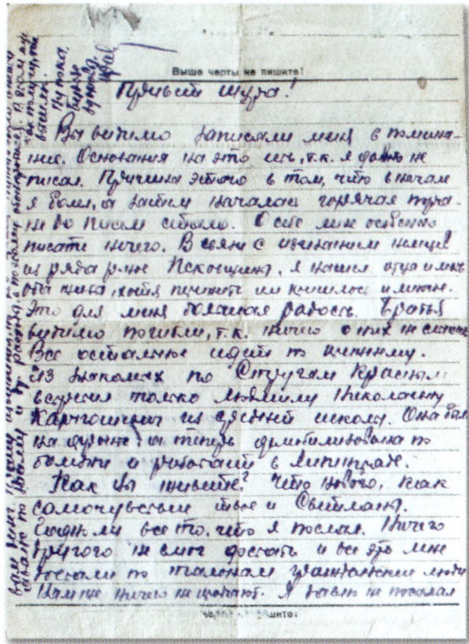

Выше черты не пишите!

Alexandra and her daughter Svetlana, in evacuation in Cheboksary.

Left, a wartime letter from Alexandra's husband, Nikolai.

Alexandra's husband Nikolai, 1964.

Alexandra, 1953.

Tea at Alexandra's.

did everything. He was very economical, a good carpenter. He built our home with his own hands.

Papa was a very good cook. We laid out a huge spread for Easter, and we kids were on the lookout for when Papa would come home, in order to receive our eggs.

We had a very, very deep well, where our ice was stored. And in the summer we made ice cream. And so, in general, we lived comfortably. We had swings, a hammock. Everything that kids could need, Papa made. He bought us new clothes, and dresses – the dressmaker Aunt Tanya sewed them for us from scratch.

So, Papa is the one who was tender to us. Papa valued us.

Alexandra's father was a railroad worker. She does not know his exact job title, since she was so young and did not delve into his work. He perished on the job during the war, struck by a train. But that was after Alexandra and her two-year-old daughter Sveta had evacuated from Leningrad Oblast, in the summer of 1941. Just two weeks after the start of the war, the fascists were on the approaches to Strugi.

On July 7, retreating troops passed through our town. Our street was completely filled by horse-drawn carts. I got my daughter into a good dress and shoes, grabbed a small saucepan, and threw a few things into a suitcase. We even crawled under the train carriages in order to get to the railway station.

Prior to this, for an entire week, they had been declaring that parents with children should leave, and they gave us evacuation papers. Well, they drove us and they fed us at every stop.

I remember a huge, huge store in Rybinsk. We hurried there and it was filled to bursting with cheese. Black walls and white cheese. For some reason, I didn't buy any cheese… And yet, when we had been back in Strugi, every last thing had been bought up. I went into a store and all that was left was bulk chocolate. I remember buying a kilogram of chocolate and we took that with us when we left.

On the road, my little Svetulya almost died. She came down with some kind of children's fit. But we rehydrated her and she recovered. I thought I would lose her. But, thank God, we made it to our destination.

Their destination, after traveling a thousand kilometers to the southeast, was on the Volga, in Chuvashia. Evacuees were unloaded from the train, put onto carts, and dispersed to villages, where they were to stay with designated families.

Locals, meanwhile, rushed to have a look at the new arrivals, unable to believe that the war was real, that it had (in this indirect way) arrived at their homes. The propaganda machine had convinced everyone that the USSR would be victorious, with very little bloodletting, all of which would be on foreign soil.

In evacuation, Alexandra exhibited surprising vitality and wisdom. She had to find some work, a place to live, and a nursery for her daughter. And all of this when the country seemed to be on the brink of death. She found work as a bookkeeper at an aviation factory and received the right to a cot in a single room along with other refugees.

The war that was supposed to end in a swift victory dragged on.

She was often hungry; the factory cafeteria served nettle soup. Thankfully, her daughter was well fed in her nursery. She and all the children were dressed in clothes sewn from remnants of parachute material. Alexandra, meanwhile, found a scrap of land and planted some vegetables. And she learned to pickle cabbage to survive the winter. And yet the freshly-arrived Muscovites and wives of officers, who landed in Chuvashia with money and produce, scornfully said that she "didn't know how to live."

When things were especially bad, Alexandra went around to nearby villages, trying to exchange her clothing for food. For her most valued possession, a wool scarf, she received a pound of butter.

And then they paid us in denatured alcohol. In Chuvashia, they really liked that stuff. We could exchange the denatured alcohol for potatoes and for flour. So gradually I became a bit better off."

The war deprived Alexandra of her father, a brother (died on the Leningrad Blockade), and a husband (who left her). But the war eventually ended, peace arrived, and the defense factory where Alexandra worked was shuttered. She was offered work at a similar plant in Azov, in the southern steppes.

And there I took up agriculture, because life was very expensive after the war. We could not buy anything other than onions and beets. So I planted corn, melons, and beans.

It was so hot there that I became as thin as a blockade survivor. I could not stand the heat. And the winter there was severe, with strong winds. The trees were covered with icicles, as if they had been decorated.

Once, I went down to the Don River for some water and the wind was so strong that I brought back less water than sand. About that time some blockade survivors – a husband and wife – arrived. It was a good family, and they said, "Girls, leave here. I will give you a recommendation letter for a construction outfit in Leningrad; they will give you a place in a dorm."

Leningrad had been Alexandra's enduring dream. Just before the war broke out, her husband found work there and the family was even allotted a room in a communal apartment, but they did not succeed in getting their residence permit in time. After the war, Leningrad was for all intents and purposes a closed city: even native Leningraders who were evacuated during the blockade found it

It was so hot there that I became as thin as a blockade survivor. I could not stand the heat.

Alexandra loves to go out onto her balcony and survey her surroundings with opera glasses.

difficult to return home. One had to amass a ton of documents, confirming that one had a place of residence and a job in Leningrad, that one had close relatives there. It was completely unrealistic for an "outsider" at the end of the 1940s to settle in the "second capital."

Nonetheless, Alexandra took the recommendation letter from the nice Leningrader and traveled north. And she succeeded in setting her hook in the city: she was given a job and a colleague permitted her to share her room. But Alexandra did not immediately receive a residency permit, and without that, she did not have a right to ration cards. So, for the first while, she had to purchase bread on the free market at astronomical prices.

Everyday problems of existence took up all of Alexandra's time and attention, and so the visage of the post-blockade city did not fix itself in her memory. But Leningrad both surprised and scared her daughter, Svetlana. When she arrived from Azov to join her mother, she saw only a blackened, destroyed city.

"The apartment question has probably been the most difficult one in my life," Alexandra admits. The state took upon itself the responsibility to guarantee living space for its workers, but receiving that space in a ravaged, post-war country was not an easy matter. More importantly, under the state-owned system, a person never became the true master of their living space, of even the miserly number of square meters allotted to them.

Over the years, Alexandra and her daughter and sister found themselves in a variety of living conditions, even for a time living in a passageway room* of a communal apartment. This sort of thing happened when several different families were settled in a single apartment. And, in order to get to one's room, one had to pass through another room. Alexandra recalls how people would just tromp through her room without even knocking, as if her living space were a public hallway.

In one instance, Alexandra was evicted: she had changed jobs and a judge sent down an order for her to evacuate her living space. So she had to scuttle between bureaucratic institutions, defending her right to have a roof over her head.

Much later, when her daughter was grown and had herself become a mother, the family lived in a luxurious (by Soviet standards) apartment, with five rooms and 54 square meters. But this was too much for three people, the powers that be decided, and so some strangers would be moved in with them. The family's autonomy was only preserved "thanks" to Alexandra's heart condition. When

---

* *Prokhodnaya komnata* – sort of a connecting room; more than a hallway, but less than a room, as one might see in palaces and larger apartments.

Alexandra's bed.

the city bureaucrats received medical certification of her diagnosis, they decided to leave her in peace and solitude.

We called this five-room apartment our House of Open Doors. Who didn't stay with us? Ballet soloists who have since left for America, for Chicago, and a singer, and a professor. And writers and journalists! Lord, who didn't we have visiting?... And so many northerners that Svetlana had met in her work.

No matter where I went on vacation, I met people that for some reason wanted to be friends with me. I brought home acquaintances from every house of rest and sanatorium.

In general, our life was always very lively, we always had people around us. I can't even count how many friends and acquaintances we had. But now I am alone. All of them have left this life...

Well into her later years, Alexandra was very active in public life. On the one hand, she had many friends, endless guests, and hours of conversations around the table with fine pastries. On the other hand, she participated in comrade courts.* In the Soviet era, this was a very widespread, "merciful" form of jurisprudence that oversaw the lowest levels of society: in worker's collectives,

* *Tovarishchesky sud* – this form of justice existed from 1961 to 1990. Members were typically elected for two years of service.

among residents of apartment complexes. On behalf of society as a whole, the comrade courts exacted punishment on lawbreakers or on citizens who were simply disorderly.

After retiring in 1973, for the next 16 years I was the secretary in a comrade court. There were lots of communal apartments, and people did not get along. Even when they were in separate apartments, people did not get along. If someone didn't like something, they would start slinging mud at someone. We had to make these people reconcile. So we did good work.

After the USSR fell apart, and the institution of people's courts no longer existed, Alexandra went on to achieve an important victory for society, or at least for her neighborhood

I fought so that there would not be a parking lot in our courtyard. They started driving both in cars and trucks – along pedestrian walkways around our building. And one of them even set up a parking space outside his window, in the trees. I fought for nature, wrote letters, and they protected our trees and were forbidden from our pathways and sidewalks. So, my actions will be remembered.

I fought for nature and they protected our trees... So my actions will be remembered.

It is also worth noting that Alexandra carefully preserves her party membership card. Revolution, Communist Party, and the Soviet Union – to her these words all belong to a higher order.

I have good feelings about the revolution. Because it became a good system. As a result, the country became more prosperous and the people were liberated from poverty. The peasants were given land so that they could work it. Factories and mills operated so that laborers could receive their pay. In general, the system worked and the country became so rich that there was no country in the world as rich as ours.

That is why the revolution was important. And even now it is important. Because now the situation is bad in Russia. Everything has again been completely destroyed. And everything needs to be raised up again.

So, I don't know, kids, your lives will be a bit difficult.

MARIA NIKOLAYEVNA RYABTSOVA
ST. PETERSBURG
14 JUNE 1917

Maria Ryabtsova has an idiosyncrasy: an easy-going inclination to laugh, combined with a certainty that life is a very difficult thing. This small, slender woman talks reluctantly about her fate, releasing stories in miserly, fragmented phrases. Her arms wrapped tightly around her chest, she sighs repeatedly, and sadly. But then sometimes, at the most unexpected moments, she will roll her head back and laugh like a young girl – irresistibly and contagiously.

Maria was born on June 14, 1917, in the village of Shulets, Rostov Uyezd, Yaroslavl Gubernia. It was not exactly a backwater, since it was not far from Moscow, at the time the second most important city in the empire. Yet it was still provincial: no industry or agriculture on a serious scale. The only things that grew well on their land were potatoes, peas, and onions.

She frowns as she recounts a story about the difficulties of village life.

We were peasants and lived in the village. Do you know where peasants work? On the land. They plow, harrow, then harvest. There was livestock. Cows and sheep, and lambs, and pigs, and piglets. There were two horses. One of them was called Lomtik ["Slice"]. He was such a good horse: he found his own way to the stable every night. Wasn't allowed, but he went anyway. He came and put his nose against the window and broke it. Mama swore at him, "Oy, what have you done!?" Yes, that was something.

The story starts off serious, but goes quickly awry when Maria reverts to a funny memory and breaks out laughing.

Early childhood images are clearly etched in Maria's memory. After her mother, her older brother was her primary caregiver and her main playmate. He mounted a box on wheels and wheeled her around. He ate her kasha (a secret they kept from their mother).

Mama asked if I had eaten up my kasha, and I replied "Sure, I ate it." But I hadn't.

She remembers noisy family holidays. Shulets had a church named for St. Nicholas, and twice each year residents of neighboring villages would come to the patron saint's holidays: Nikolai's Winter and Nikolai's Summer.*

There were so many guests – oy, oy, oy! Mama had lots of brothers and they all came. You couldn't get into the yard because of all the horses and carts or sleds. So many people and all of them needed a place to sleep. We had just one room in our house, so at night everyone nestled together on the floor. And there were small children rocking in slings hung from the rafters.

This memory is likely from the 1920s, because by the following decade the battle against religion and the Church was well underway in the Soviet Union.

There were small children rocking in slings hung from the rafters.

Maria can't recall if any of her relatives or friends suffered from the repressions or dekulakizations of the 1920s and 1930s. By all accounts, the family lived very modestly, if not in poverty. And it would not have been possible to call them kulaks.† Modest peasants like her family were generally untouched, so long as they quickly joined the kolkhoz, without any bickering or bargaining.

As soon as I could walk, I was put to work. Mama went into the fields, and we, the little ones, worked in the garden. I was still rather small when I began working like a grown up. Harvesting the rye or wheat with a sickle. One had to work, to earn workdays. Had to have something to eat. Wasn't much, but we still got something for a workday in the kolkhoz.

They didn't pay cash wages in the kolkhoz, but for each workday, a hash mark ("palka") was put down in a special journal. If the work was particularly difficult, one might receive two marks; if the work was light, just half a mark. And then, when the harvest was brought in, grain or vegetables would be distributed based on the number of workdays one had accumulated. But if the harvest was bad, then the kolkhoz workers got nothing.

Another difficult part was that kolkhoz workers and their families also had to buy clothing, shoes, soap, salt, sugar, tea and other "everyday goods." As Maria puts it, "Shoes don't grow out of the earth." So, aside from the required kolkhoz work, one had to grow things in one's own garden parcel, or perhaps raise a pig. Then take it to market and sell it – for rubles, not workdays.

Maria's parents nonetheless found a way to send their daughter to school.

---

* The saint's two important holidays are December 6 and May 9 (Old Style).

† See footnote, page page 92.

Maria's father and his sons from his first marriage.
Petrograd, 1914

Maria in her youth.

I entered the first grade at eight. Didn't have a notebook. We wrote on pieces of slate, then we'd wipe them off and write again. For lunch, we'd bring along a piece of bread. Didn't have a bag, just wrapped it up in a scarf.

She studied for five years in all, which wasn't bad for those times – many stopped after just two or three years. But after five years her studies ended. She had to help her mother and father.

Her parents, Vera and Nikolai, died at the end of the 1930s – they were each about 65 years old. Her father passed first and then her mother, having just succeeded in marrying Maria off.

Maria remembers how her parents were in their old age.

Papa was calm, and Mama was stricter. Mama had thin, grey hair. Papa's hair was black, with flecks of grey. Mama had no teeth, but Papa had some – he took all his teeth to the grave.

Mama had no teeth, but Papa had some – he took all his teeth to the grave.

Maria's husband, Nikolai Ryabtsov, was a city boy who worked in the Rostov city government. He came to Shulets on some sort of business and stopped at Maria's house to ask for some milk. In 1938 he took his young wife back to Rostov, a small but very ancient Russian town.*

Back then, you know, everyone was only leaving, leaving the village. Why leave? It was the times. But we lived in the countryside a bit. Buried Mama and then left for Rostov. I was married, so of course I went. He didn't want to live in the village.

The Ryabtsovs had two sons, and 1941 was a catastrophic year for the family. Her husband went off to war, and Maria was left alone with two small children in a city toward which the front line was rapidly moving.

My two children died at the start of the war. They were with me... One of them was two, the other six months. It's because I had no money, no work, nothing to eat.

She sighs sadly and stares into the distance. But her voice does not shake, which is somewhat eerie. Time heals, but in this instance mercilessly. She can only remember the name of one of her sons. Yuri. The second she has forgotten.

Then I found some work. The city was not large, after all, and there were not many companies. But there was a factory that wove things. Previously, we had had a chickory factory. There were just a few factories like that. So where are you going to find work? I worked in a sewing shop. It closed up during the war. The war began in June, and they turned the primary-secondary school into a big hospital and started hiring people there. So I went and worked there the entire war. I was so happy that they took me on. To be able to go to work, to have something to live on.

---

* Rostov Veliky, northeast of Moscow, not to be confused with Rostov-on-Don which is in the country's South.

Maria celebrates at her 100th birthday party.

Maria notes (without offense or complaint) that in fact she was only paid half her salary. The other half was sent to support the front. This was a common practice during the war, and certainly such contributions were not always given voluntarily. But here is an indisputable fact: the contributions of simple Soviet citizens were used to build entire tank columns, aviation fleets, and warships mobilized against Fascism.

The front did not reach Yaroslavl Oblast, which is a bit north and east of Moscow. Yet it still was not easy for workers in the rear: they lived half-starved and did the work of three. Still, it was easier for them than for civilians on territory where fighting was taking place or that was under German occupation.

Yes, there were warnings. But not many. When the Germans approached Moscow, there was some talk [about the front approaching]. But they did not reach us. There were times when someone cried out, "Warning! Warning!" And we took the patients to the basement. But there were not many, because the Germans were immediately pushed back.

Maria calmly recounts her husband's return, as if he had not been fighting for four years, but was late coming home from work.

The war ended, of course, and he returned. Our apartment building was two stories, and we lived on the second floor. He knocked on the gutter pipe, the way he always used to knock when he arrived home a bit late. And I opened the door for him.

But Nikolai was only home on leave, not for good. After the victory, he was called to serve abroad, on territory occupied by the Soviet army.

So he said, "You wanna come with?"

"Of course I'll go."

And off we went!

The Ryabtsovs lived abroad for two years. Where exactly, Maria does not remember.

In German territory or someplace won from the Germans. Poles lived in some parts.

Their son Vladimir was born there in 1946, in a small military village. But it was forbidden to register his birth abroad, so they took him back to the Soviet Union.

My son was very small, wrapped up in a blanket. In Rybinsk there was a stop, several hours. We went to a restaurant – it was the first time in my life.

In Rostov, a second child was born soon thereafter – her daughter Vera. Maria gave birth to her at home, because she did not have time to get to the birthing home.

Would have had to run there on foot. But running was a bit difficult with such a belly. Couldn't make it. A babushka helped out – she'd been visiting from the village.

A younger Maria, seated at left, with her husband Nikolai and children Vladimir and Vera, and a relative (standing in rear), in the late 1940s or early 1950s.

While my husband went looking for a car to take me there, the babushka did everything. She knew everything, since she bore 12 kids of her own.

About two years later, Maria's brother, who had settled in Leningrad, wrote her a letter: "Move here, there is plenty of work." And in the spring of 1950, after the weather turned, the family picked up and moved to the northern capital. They settled in a workers' village on the outskirts, and Nikolai found work in a construction organization.

Post-war Leningrad was being rapidly rebuilt; new residential areas and micro-rayons sprung up like mushrooms after a rain.

At first, there were small homes. Then they tore those down to make the bigger ones. And here, in our Okhta, when we arrived, there was a barnyard and a pigsty. Now a theater stands there.*

In 1961, the family moved to its own apartment in a five-story building that her husband had helped build – a typical "khrushchyovka." This is what they called the standard, multi-story, cement-paneled buildings raised on a mass scale in the USSR under Nikita Khrushchev. The buildings were cheap and planned as temporary housing, but to this day people all across the country live in them.

When they moved into the apartment, the walls were painted a dreary, dark color, and the parquet floors were spattered with paint, because the painters had done their work so quickly and sloppily. Maria complained that she had to scrape the paint from the parquet because it would not wash off.

Yet life was nothing like it had been before or even during the war: a separate apartment, a job in the big city. For almost 15 years, Maria worked as a drill operator in a factory, but in her labor book one reads a wide range professions: nurse, mill operator, storekeeper, cloakroom attendant, seamstress.

The children went to school, the family was well fed. But things were still tight when it came to clothing.

The lines for shoes were so long... They yelled: "C'mon, go faster, get in line!" They'd write down numbers, walk along, verify them. You stand and stand, and you get nothing. Myself, I sewed dresses, skirts, bedsheets. But the difficult sewing jobs I gave to dressmakers. If it was good fabric, wool or silk, we'd give it to dressmakers. There was no material, we also stood in line for that, whether we got it or not. We cherished a weekend dress. And for what? They hang there, the cherished dresses. But still, there is nothing to wear.

---

* A historic region of the city, on the right bank of the Neva, so named because it is located where the Okhta river meets the Neva.

To this day, Maria lives in the same two-room apartment into which she and husband Nikolai moved half a century ago. Her grandson Alexander and his wife Natalia live there as well.

Maria's husband long ago left this world, but the family has grown, the relatives have multiplied, and they come around to visit their old grandma.

Actually, for her age, Maria has a rather active social life. She has a girlfriend who is just three years younger, and they often get together or speak on the phone.

Several times Maria repeats how at night she often wakes up and remembers her past. It's long, she says, and there is plenty to remember. But it was difficult, not like now. And yet it seems that Maria is a person who lives in the present, not in the past. Daily tasks perk her up, and her voice becomes stronger, more certain. She can get to the stores on her own, she makes her own meals, and she keeps a watchful eye on the family pet: a gigantic snail.

In the winter, Maria fell sick with bronchitis – the first time in her life that she ever had a serious illness. The doctor, examining her, said it was nothing to worry about, that elderly people often get it, that it would pass. Maria, who had no experience with being sick, could not understand why she suddenly was feeling so poorly. But she turned the corner reasonably quickly, and was soon back on her feet, bustling about the apartment and joking with her grandchildren.

Maria asleep in her bed.

THE DOUBLE PORTRAITS

In the course of this project, photographer Mikhail Mordasov invented and perfected a system for the creation of live double portraits. Using only creative lighting, a tripod, and a plate of ordinary glass, he was able (with a few assistants) to create merged images of the centenarians and one of their relatives. (No photoshop or other post-processing wizardry was used; images were captured in a single frame.) The images that resulted are telling demonstrations of familial resemblance and the passage of time.

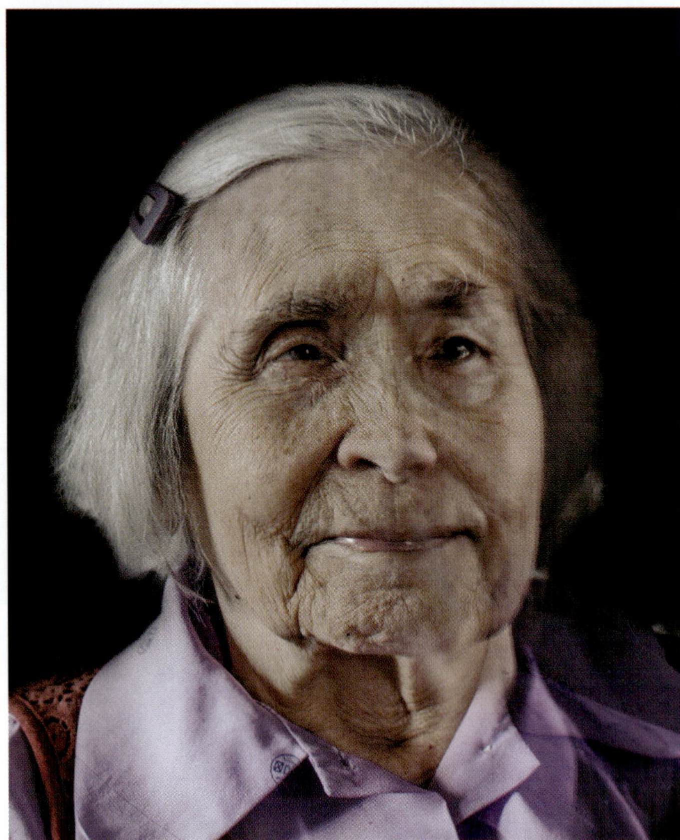

Left: Centenarian Galina Grebneva.
Right: Her daughter Irina.

Right: Centenarian Alexandra Antonova.
Left: Her daughter Svetlana.

In the making of the double portraits, the two relatives actually sit facing one another in a blackened room. Only one half of each person's face is illuminated, then, through some careful manipulation of light and reflections, their two half-portraits are merged into a single image in camera.

Right: Centenarian Saima Ritalahti
Left: Her granddaughter Pia.

Right: Centenarian Maria Rylik.
Left: Her granddaughter Yuliya.

Left: Centenarian Leopold Damiecki.
Right: His great-grandson Marcin.

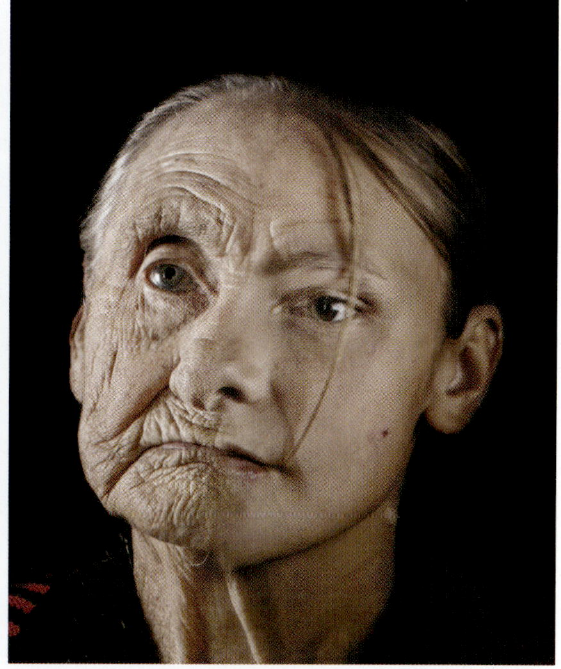

Left: Centenarian Lyudmila Pakhomova.
Right: Her great-granddaughter Alexandra.

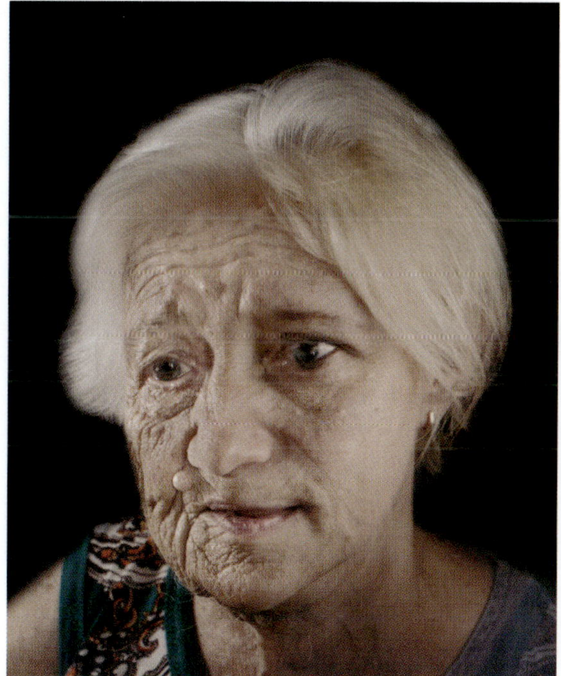

Left: Centenarian Lidiya Motina.
Right: Her granddaughter Svetlana.

Left: Centenarian Maria Konyayeva.
Right: Her daughter Galina.

MARIA VASILYEVNA YEVSTAFEVA
OSTROVKI VILLAGE, PSKOV OBLAST
16 JUNE 1917

Maria Yevstafeva is in a bad way: she is departing. For the few weeks prior to her interview, she was considerably more active. She was reading and living as active a life as would seem possible for someone who is 100 years old and paraplegic. But now she has completely given up. Any contact with the outside world is difficult for her. She does not hear well, and speaks poorly, swallowing words and whole sentences as she speaks.

Valentina, her daughter, rests her in a seated position on her bed with very little effort – so thin and light is the elderly woman. She tucks a thick blanket around her and places before her a coffee table with a mound of three large pillows set atop it. The reason for this construction becomes clear a few minutes later, after the interview begins. Maria tires so quickly that, after speaking for a bit, she slowly lowers her entire body onto the pillows to rest.

It is as if every day I remember how I lived, and then I start to think, no.

Her recollections come in short bursts, and when she summons forth her stories, she often mixes dreams with reality. But the short stories are dramatic and chilling.

She was born Maria Leonova on June 16, 1917, in the village of Noglovo, in Sebezh Uyezd, Vitebsk Gubernia. Today, this is just six miles from the Russian border with Latvia. She lived there for some 90 years, until she was the village's last living resident. Then her daughter moved her to live with her in Ostrovki – a village of nearly the same size, only 100 kilometers to the east.

What sort of cards does Fate deal a person, if they live their entire life in remote forests on the outskirts of an empire?

I did not go to school, I am not educated. I went to first grade, they sewed me a dress with a pocket and bought me a pencil. I put the pencil in my pocket, but lost it during the first school break, the big one. I even remember my first teacher. I lost my pencil and no one at home gave me money for a new one. They said, "No more studies. You'll tend the geese at home." So I tended the geese. And we had a lot of geese. My parents were well-off, they were. I worked at home alongside my father. We plowed and reaped together. My parents were peasants, hard workers. My father was a real slogger.

She recalls how her older brother, Trofim, was repressed. He was a bookkeeper, and on November 30, 1937, he was arrested and sentenced to 10 years in the camps on the most "popular" of the criminal codes from that era: Article 58, for "counter-revolutionary activity." Some four million souls were sentenced under Article 58 during Stalin's reign.

This spare bit of information about Trofim was gleaned from the public database of Soviet victims of political repression. Maria offers a more poignant account:

Poor fellow, he was the first to join the kolkhoz. There were muzhiks in the village and they were chatting. And he let slip a few words or other against those in charge. Three of his enemies collaborated and wrote a denunciation. That very night a "Black Raven" came and took him away. And they sent him to Siberia; he worked in forestry. Such a child! He'd just married, had a daughter... And then, when they released all those sorts of prisoners, they sent all his documents to the militia post: a death notice, he died from hunger. I received the documents and sent them to his daughter. How happy she was to receive her father's documents! And the people who had written the denunciation of him, they went off to work for the Germans during the war.*

On the eve of war, Maria fell madly in love with a man named Karp Nikitin, but it was an unlucky love. Thoughts of it torment her to this day.

I myself don't know how it happened. Oh, my reckless youth... I wouldn't wish on anyone the sort of love I felt for him. I would have laid down my life for him. I wanted to see him, to hear him, every minute. He went into the army for three years, and I said "You get out of the army, and you want to marry, I will. If you don't, I won't marry anyone."

While her beloved Karp was in the army, they corresponded. But it turns out that her letters were intercepted, read, and hidden by a certain Katyenka, who worked at the local post office, and quite possibly was a competitor for Karp's affections. Katyenka also wrote to Karp all sorts of nonsense about Maria that was harmful to the couple's relationship.

---

* *Chyorny Voron*, commonly translated as "Black Maria." This was the infamous black sedan outfitted for hauling prisoners and suspects away for questioning, jail, or prison.

Maria with Karp, whom she loved beyond measure.

Ostrovki village.

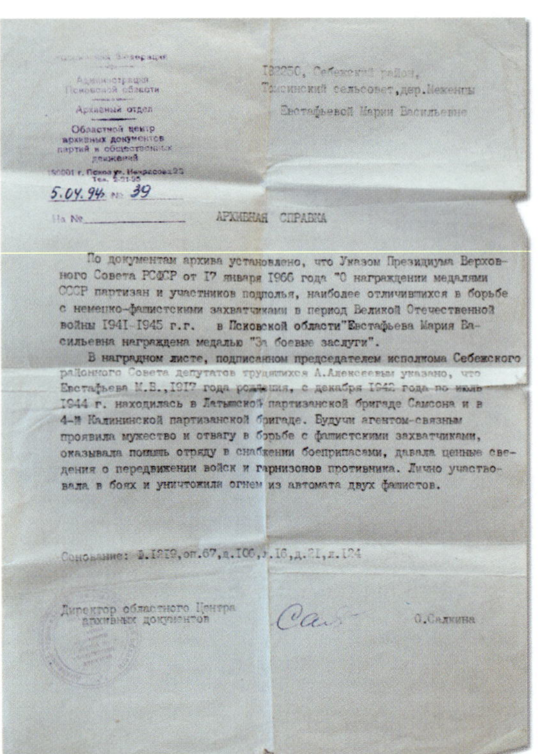

[illegible] Федерация

Администрация Псковской области

Архивный отдел

Областной центр архивных документов партий и общественных движений

180001 г. Псков ул. Некрасова 23
Тел. 2-21-95

5.04.94 № 39

На №

I82250, Себежский район,
Томсинский сельсовет, дер. Меженцы

Евстафьевой Марии Васильевне

АРХИВНАЯ СПРАВКА

По документам архива установлено, что Указом Президиума Верховного Совета РСФСР от I7 января I966 года "О награждении медалями СССР партизан и участников подполья, наиболее отличившихся в борьбе с немецко-фашистскими захватчиками в период Великой Отечественной войны I94I-I945 г.г. в Псковской области" Евстафьева Мария Васильевна награждена медалью "За боевые заслуги".

В наградном листе, подписанном председателем исполкома Себежского районного Совета депутатов трудящихся А.Алексеевым указано, что Евстафьева М.В., I9I7 года рождения, с декабря I942 года по июль I944 г. находилась в Латышской партизанской бригаде Самсона и в 4-й Калининской партизанской бригаде. Будучи агентом-связным проявила мужество и отвагу в борьбе с фашистскими захватчиками, оказывала помощь отряду в снабжении боеприпасами, давала ценные сведения о передвижении войск и гарнизонов противника. Лично участвовала в боях и уничтожила огнем из автомата двух фашистов.

Основание: Ф.I9I9, оп.67, д.I06, т.I6, д.2I, л.I24

Директор областного Центра архивных документов — О.Салкина

An official letter attesting to the fact that Maria aided the partisans during the second World War.

Slippers and a broom at the entrance to Maria's home.

Karp returned from the army to the village, but a month later World War II started and he was called up. Whether the young couple succeeded in getting married or not is an open question. Maria does not herself call Karp her husband, but as to her relationship with him, she says:

There was happiness in life, when I was married for the first time: to my beloved just before the war.

But her daughter Valentina clarifies that theirs was an unofficial marriage.

After the war, Karp did not return to the village, and the official Yevstafev family version is that he disappeared in the war without a trace. Maria, very agitated and visibly upset, recounts a dream. In truth, it could be a real memory that, with the passage of years, now only seems like a dream.

And so I had this dream. Vivid as life. I'm standing on a street and a man and a woman are standing near me. Middle-aged. I don't know them. And we are talking. And I can tell that this man is from Leningrad. I say, "Young man, tell me about Karp. Did he return from the war?" He gave me this malicious smirk. He says, "Got married, I think to some Belarusan or other." And the woman, she says to me, "Ugh, you forget about him. Don't regret it. He's just like his father." And his father beat his first wife to death. So then it became easier for me. I forgot about that unlucky love. Our thing ended, and I don't know where he is. Maybe he is living in Leningrad.

Beginning in 1939, Maria worked as a telephone operator in the village post office. She was at work when the war began; she secured communications within the region until the lines were cut. But the fascists occupied the region in the second week of the war, and their occupation lasted more than three years.

When the Germans approached her village, Maria and some other young women at first hid in the forest. Her mother and mother-in-law refused to leave. "They won't touch us old folks," they said. But, in fact, the fascists shot them. They also shot Maria's sister and niece – one was 6, the other 4 – because the head of their family had joined the partisans. He too was eventually hunted down and hung.

One of Maria's brother's died at the front. The other died in the blockade of Leningrad.

Eventually, Maria came out of hiding and worked as a peasant in occupied territory. The fascists had imposed an in-kind tax on all peasants, such that every family was required to contribute to the food reserves of Hitler's army.

But Maria also had a second, secret life. She helped the partisans: securing produce, obtaining information, carrying out espionage, recruiting new members to partisan brigades.

There was this episode. A young boy and girl were sent from the front to organize a demolition group. To blow up bridges and trains. They came to live with us and they lived like husband and wife. They were so young: Vanya and Granya. And how do you go about organizing a demolition group? There were still plenty of young men who had not been drafted for the war. So I take a bus to Sebezh. And I sit on the bus and see one of these kids sitting there. I sit next to him and I say, "Young man, are you still interested in fighting?" I look at his feet. He asks, "Fight, how?" And I explain that a group of demolitionists has infiltrated here and that it wants to organize a brigade on this route. He says, "I'll think about it. We have some other guys." And so I connected them with Granya and Vanya. And they created a demolition group and bombed a train.

Maria preserves a small piece of torn paper. It is about one-eighth the size of a piece of ruled notebook paper. It is a certificate, signed by a partisan commander, confirming that Maria helped them. And in the regional archive there is yet another certificate. It notes that Maria personally shot two fascists. But she does not talk about that.

He came and he hypnotized both me and my family. And he took me home with him.

In 1944, when Pskov Oblast was liberated, Maria was promoted to head of the communications division in the neighboring, slightly larger village. She worked there, she says, "for 38 years and 8 months in one position, without any bad marks." This, of course, in addition to her agricultural activity. Maria always had a cow and piglets, and harvested hay for the cattle and kept a garden. She never took a vacation, only occasionally visiting relatives in Leningrad or Riga. And she has only been in a hospital twice: both times while giving birth to her children.

Maria named them Valya and Tanya, in honor of the nieces who were viciously murdered in 1941. Yet today she cannot exactly remember why she chose these names. But she does remember well the story of her second husband, Vasily Yerofeyevich, who was nine years her junior.

I would never have married him. But it happened. He came and hypnotized both me and my family. And he took me home with him. He did not say why he took me. Was it for marriage or, as I thought, to work at his place? He grabbed me, took me in his arms, and hauled me into his hut. And put me on the bed. His mother and sister were lying on the stove. And he lay with me there in that bed. So that's how I got married, may God save and preserve me. I would never in my life have married him if he had not deceived the whole family in that way. Then my brother came the next day. To get me, probably. I didn't agree, and kept living with Yerofeyevich, in order not to disgrace him or me. And Valya and then Tanya was born.

She recounts this story in the presence of her daughter and granddaughter, which rather embarrasses, perhaps even offends them. Maria complains that she lived alone for 70 years, plowing and mowing all by herself, and everything

Maria and Vasily – the man who "hypnotized her," and became her husband – and their daughter Valentina. 1950s.

Maria and her great-granddaughter Maria.

Maria and her cat.

was just fine. But as soon as her daughter brought her to live with her, her legs stopped working. Prior to that, she read a lot. Her daughter Valentina would bring her books from the village library. But, after Maria became paralyzed, she decided that the books she had previously been reading were ridiculous, and she now reads only religious literature.

Maria says that if her legs were working, she'd hop up right now and go out and cut down all the grass in the yard and garden with her scythe. She's never been happy with how her daughter takes care of the place. Yet Valentina is now caring for the third person in her life to be bedridden: this is how her mother-in-law and husband both died.

Valentina is a calm woman. She speaks quietly and silently cares for the house. Perhaps it is just her temperament, but more likely she is simply worn down from taking care of her mother and their little village farm, which cannot be easy at her age.

Irina, Valentina's daughter and Maria's granddaughter, is a tiny young woman with a tender but slightly frightened gaze. She was born here, in the village, and stayed here to live, deciding not to abandon her aging mother and grandmother. Despite her fragile physique, Irina easily turns and sets her grandmother on the bed.

Neither in mother nor daughter does one sense any resentment or bitterness that this old, immobile person is taking up their time and energy.

Maria, however, is very tired of living.

I wouldn't wish anyone to live to this age. And to not be able to die. That is suffering. I would be happy to die.

ANTONINA ALEXANDROVNA KUSLEYEVA
VELIKY NOVGOROD
26 JUNE 1917

Antonina Kusleyeva is a very restless centenarian. If she does not need to be posing for a photo or recounting her history on camera, she gets up from her chair and hurries off to deal with some unavoidable domestic matter. Maybe she is checking to make sure the table is properly filled with food for guests, or she is looking for the cat who has hidden from the same guests, or perhaps she is going in search of the family photo album and the plastic bag that contains her labor medals.

Her daughter, Galina, complains about her strong-willed mother, about her stubbornness. In part, this is because Antonina's eyes and ears are failing her. And, afraid of losing the thread of the conversation, she repeatedly asks what her daughter has said. Antonina passionately wants to tell her life story herself, and, seizing the moment, she begins a long, emotional monologue.

We lived in Nordovka, I was born there. Nordovka is a fine village, very fine, actually. It's in Bashkiria. It was all Russians there.

Antonina's hometown is 150 kilometers south of Ufa, the capital of modern Bashkiria. In 1917, the area was in Orenburg Gubernia. Nordovka is actually not far from the symbolic border between Europe and Asia, on fertile plains with a warm climate. It had long been Bashkir land, but after the emancipation of the serfs in 1861, peasants from poorer, more overpopulated regions of Russia came here in search of a better life. Nordovka was founded at the end of the nineteenth century by several Russian families who purchased some land from locals.

I know that grampa built the church there. He lived to 115, grampa did. And probably I come from him. I will soon be 100. Oh, Lord! That church still stands in Nordovka, Galya has seen it on the computer. They say that wooden churches are built without a single nail.

Both of Antonina's parents were from Nordovka.

They lived in the same village. They played together, went outside together. They didn't date. They simply knew each other. And when it was time to find her a husband, she didn't know who the groom would be. Her parents arranged it all. And when they stood together beneath the crown, she looks at him, "Oh, it's Kapustin!" She was so happy. She liked him and he liked her. And they were married. Then I was born. But when I was six months old my father died in the revolution. I don't remember him. But I feel sad for him. What change did the revolution bring? Could it have been pleasant for parents to lose their son? Grandma suddenly went deaf. I was a baby, still alive, but I was left without a father. Could that have been pleasant for them?*

Antonina does not know the details surrounding the death of her father, Nikolai Feoktistovich Kapustin. But archives with information on the village's history contain a description of the tragic events. In the summer of 1918, when civil war was churning in Russia, counter-revolutionary riots took place in Orenburg Gubernia. In Nordovka, 36 Red Army soldiers and members of revolutionary committees were executed. A certain Nikolai Kapustin was among them.

The family has a blurry photograph of young Nikolai, looking every inch a stereotypical Red Army soldier from the Civil War era. It is all that Antonina has to remember her father by, for even her last name is that of her stepfather, Kusleyeva.

When Father died, Mama went to Aktyubinsk,† but I was left behind. She worked on plantations there, and I lived with her brother, at Uncle Styopa's. Then, when I turned seven, she came for me. She took me to Dzhambul,‡ in Kazakhstan, and there she married a man with four kids. He was 19 years older than her. Well, we lived quietly like that. He was a watchman, but she had been wooed by an agronomist. Later, when I was grown, I says to her, "Why did you marry that old man? Why not the agronomist? That would have been a husband! I could have had a brother and a

---

* A central part of the Orthodox marriage ceremony is the placing of crowns over the heads of the bride and groom. This is why a Russian Orthodox wedding is called a "crowning."

† Today, Aktobe, which is south of Orenburg Gubernia, and is located in Kazakhstan.

‡ Present-day Taraz, Kazakhstan, the oldest city in the country, located near its southern border with Kirgizia.

sister!" But she married herself off to some sort of... Lord! He was a watchman! Mama was beautiful, very beautiful.

To this day, Antonina holds a grudge that her stepfather did not treat her like one of his own. One night she woke up and saw her stepfather doling out his pocket change to his four children. But to little tow-haired Tonya he gave not a single kopek.

I grew up without a father. And you know what my stepfather called me? I had white hair, so he said, "Whitey." I was a good student, but his kids did not study. They didn't get past second grade. And he says, "Whitey won't be holding a shovel." And I finished five grades, I was literate. I loved math. Ooo! How I loved math. I loved to solve problems, oh, did I love that. My teacher really respected, liked me. Then, when I finished five grades, stepfather says, "I am not sending you for more schooling." So what was I to do? I entered the FZU, learned to be a telegraph operator.*

Meanwhile, her relatives who stayed behind in Bashkiria fell victim to the Stalin-era repressions.

Mama's sister married a rich man. They had four children, and there was the two of them. And they were not lazy. They had cattle. They kept pigs, birds, cows. They worked the land. They had plenty of everything. That whole village was full of rich people. But they were all dekulakized and sent to Siberia. But were they really kulaks? They lived off their work... They didn't hire any laborers. They did the work themselves, and they sent them to Siberia. To Prokopyevsk. They took them and dumped them in the forest. "Live however you like," they said. They dug holes in the ground and made their homes. There were lots of nuts there. In Siberia, there were lots of nuts. They lived on nuts. And still, they again became rich. They found work, and they worked. They worked the land and again built homes. And again they became well off, and lived well. But what sort of kulaks were they, if they lived well and worked? Hunger and cold, they saw it all. And what they earned, it was all taken away, all of it.

Were they really kulaks? They did the work themselves, and they sent them to Siberia.

Even though it was not safe to be in contact with kulaks and repressed persons, they stayed in touch. Later, when Antonina was grown and had children of her own, she traveled to the Urals to visit her aunt's family.

After finishing her education as a telegraph operator, Antonina received her work dispensation.† She was sent to a remote region of eastern Kazakhstan, near the border with China, to the recently built village of Aktogay. It was an

---

* *Fabrichno-Zavodskoe Uchenichestvo* – the lowest ranking of technical schools in the Soviet era, these were institutions connected to factories.

† In the Soviet era, upon completing education, graduates were sent, or assigned, to work for three years where the school and factory bosses decided they ought to be sent.

Antonina in school. She is second from the right in the second row, with flowers in her lap.

Antonina's mother and father.

important junction on the newly completed rail line connecting Siberia and the Soviet republics in Central Asia.

There I worked, and there I got married. He was the head bookkeeper for a railroad administration department. Gave birth to four kids. The second, a boy, died at 10 months. But the other three lived. Well, grew up normal. My husband behaved very badly. I endured and endured it, and then I left. Left for Dzhambul. Then on June 22, the war began. And I was there with three kids... I got a job at the train station. First as a platform controller. Had a good boss at the station, a Tatar woman. She and I had been friends since childhood. She got me the job there.

Antonina's daughter Galina recalls how for a long time it was impossible to get Antonina's ex-husband to pay alimony. After the divorce, he set up with a new family and even had more children. So one of Antonina's friends advised her to write a letter of complaint to Shvernik.

Today, this name is forgotten by all by a few, yet in the mid-1940s to early 1950s, Nikolai Shvernik was Chairman of the Presidium of the Supreme Soviet – formally speaking the head of the Soviet state, on par with western governments' presidents. Of course, the position was largely ceremonial, and Shvernik was merely a shadow of the real ruler, Communist Party General Secretary Josef Stalin. Not until Leonid Brezhnev assumed this position in 1977 (for the second time; the first time was under Khrushchev), was the post of president combined with General Secretary.

To this day, Galina is surprised that her mother's letter to the Kremlin had such an immediate and real effect. Within a month of sending the letter, alimony payments started showing up.

The most difficult time was during the war. During the war, there was hunger and cold.

At that time, Antonina's household was comprised of five women: three daughters, her mother, and herself. In other words, four dependents and one worker.

They gave us 200 grams of bread for the children. And 200 for Mama. And 400 for me. They didn't give us anything else. Nothing but bread. We were very hungry. We ate grass, we ate the horses' sorrel. We ate everything, God forbid. And, working during the war as a cashier in the baggage room, we would work a 24-hour shift, and then the next day they would send us to work on the kolkhoz. We needed to weed everything, to harvest the grass. Then, in the fall, we harvested corn. Beets we harvested too. We did everything, even hauling gravel to the platform. And then the men packed the gravel into bags and sent it to the front lines, to build barricades. That's how it was all through the war. We got no vacation and worked 24-hour shifts.

Working on the railway, Antonina watched trains with new recruits traveling west, and hospital trains with the injured traveling east.

The soldiers went off to the front... But when the hospital trains came back, the soldiers were without arms or legs. Hanging in cradles. They were going to Siberia to their parents. Oy, God forbid. That should never happen. The poor servicemen, poor soldiers.

Looking through her photo album, Kisleyeva stumbles across a completely forgotten "echo of the war." It is a photograph about the size of a postage stamp, showing a beautiful, well-dressed young woman. On the back side are just two words: "Hello Antonina!" It was sent her as a keepsake by a woman evacuated to Kazakhstan from European Russia during the war and who was given shelter in their home. Sixty years on, no one can remember the woman's name.

Galina, remembering her childhood, confirms that things were not entirely difficult for her mother. Her grandmother raised them and took care of the household, and from time to time one or two of the girls were sent to live with their father. Her mother "just" had to go to work each day.

For a moment, Antonina returns to the workdays in her youth, when she worked as a station announcer.

Attention! Attention! Train number 101, for example, Novosibirsk-Moscow, is arriving on track number one. Departing passengers be careful. Go to the platform. Sit in the train car. Train number such and such is arriving on track number one. The stop is 15 minutes long. Be careful.

I was so young, I had a fine voice. Everyone said, "Oy! How well she does the announcements!" But now I am already an old woman, you can't understand anything I say.

Antonina describes her work by saying, "I sat with a pen and wrote." These days, we call such work, often with a light tone of contempt, office work. Yet Antonina was the first in her family's many generations of peasants who did not experience the difficult, exhausting life of working the land. And it is the basis for a certain amount of pride, both for her and for all three of her daughters: Lyubov, Lilia, and Galina, who all received good educations.

There is actually an interesting story in that realm, connected with the daughters' school in Dzhambul. Studies were going well there, as they ought in a fine school. All the teachers had a good command of their subjects and loved their students. But then, suddenly, in 1958, one after another the teachers began to leave. The children were alternately surprised and upset. Only sometime later was it learned that all of these excellent teachers, all of these highly-educated, intelligent people, had been exiles. At the height of the Stalinist repressions of the 1930s, they had been sent away from the capital, to someplace on the empire's

Antonina in 1936, with friends. She is front, left.

"What do I have to complain about? I have everything."

edge, to southern Kazakhstan. And in 1958, five years after Stalin's death, when the Thaw was in full swing, they were finally allowed to return home.

Incidentally, the writer Alexander Solzhenitsyn was exiled to Dzhambul Oblast during this same period. He worked in a village school as a teacher of math and physics.

The happiest day was when they gave me a free vacation package to Sochi. I don't remember the year. We had a great vacation. Oy, it was so good, they fed us so well. They took us to concerts, to the theater. We rested an entire month. It was so good. There were dances in the square. We swam. I am a good swimmer, I can float on my back in the water. I can lie right on the water. One time I lay like that for a long time, and floated a long, long way away, so I would be far from everyone. Then I see some fellow swimming over and he says, "How do you do that? I have been watching you for a long time." And I say, "You need to have good balance. And then you will never drown."

You need to have good balance. And then you will never drown.

In the mid-1970s, Antonina and her mother left Kazakhstan, where they had spent over half a century of their lives, and moved from the empire's southern reaches to its northwest corner, to Novgorod. Her youngest daughter Galina had settled in the city – sent there for her first work assignment after the institute, and she was raising her son alone. Thus did life come full circle, and Antonina moved in with her daughter to help raise her grandchildren.

Since then, Antonina has barely changed her place of residence. There was a time when she tried to move to Ukraine, but she couldn't get used to life there, so she returned to Novgorod.

What do I have to complain about? I can't complain. Why? I have everything. They give me a pension. What is there to complain about? Putin is very good. Medvedev is good. May they be healthy. I get a pension of 17,000. Five I give to Galya, so that she can pay for the apartment. And the rest I keep to buy groceries, whatever I need. What else? I've lived to 100. What's to complain about?...

If only there was no more war, no wars ever again. But these Americans, they've got something up their nose. They all don't like Russia, Russia is bad. Russia does not offend anyone, it helps everyone. If everyone just got along peacefully, it would be good. If they just worked the land. Were friends with everyone, with all peoples. No one would be hurt. Not children, not adults, not old people. And it would be good. If only we lived together peacefully, as before. True?

SAIMA RITAHLAHTI

TAMPERE, FINLAND
26 JUNE 2017

In the center of Tampere, Finland's second largest city (and perhaps its most left-leaning*), the iconic Tampella factory sits astride a man-made channel, connecting two lakes that differ in height by 18 meters. This geological gift provided the town with hydropower that made industrial development possible here in the 1800s. Indeed, Tampella was once a thriving manufacturer of paper machines, locomotives, and military weaponry. This played a large part in the city being nicknamed "the Manchester of the North." Today the factory has been repurposed into museums, shops, and offices.

Saima Ritahlahti worked in the Tampella factory from when she was 17, then labored in a string of other mills for the rest of her working life. But not as you'd know it by outward appearances. Elegant and poised in her gold teardrop earrings and smart, blue linen suit, she looks neither like someone who turned 100 years six months ago (75, perhaps), nor like a person spent from long years as a millworker. In fact, until two years ago she would regularly go out to a dance club, where her friends would ask if she was there looking for a man ("I answered that I could find men elsewhere as well," she quips). With little prompting, she and her daughter waltz around the room like whirling dervishes.

---

* It was here on November 1, 1905, during a general strike, that workers published the famous Red Declaration (because of the paper it was printed on), which called for the Senate of Finland to resign; it demanded universal suffrage, freedom of assembly, and freedom of association. It also had the gall to ask for an end to censorship. In addition, it was in this city, in 1905, that Vladimir Lenin met Joseph Stalin for the first time. Lenin lived here for two years before leaving the Russian Empire for Western Europe in 1907 (then returning in 1917 with German aid).

Saima in the 1930s.

Delousing in an army sauna before going home. Saima's husband Maono is standing in the center, holding the pan.

Wedding photo of Saima's parents.

Saima's hair is cropped stylishly short, and her eyes are piercingly blue. She alternately laughs and cries while recounting her memories, rocking slowly in a comfortable chair in the living room of her daughter's quiet suburban home, surrounded by energetic family members, including her daughter, son-in-law, granddaughter, and great-grandson. She has a chronic medical issue with her esophagus, as a result of which she must now take all her meals through a feeding tube, and because of which she is occasionally overcome by coughing fits.

Born Saima Starck in a sauna* in the town of Kokemäki, just to the south and west of Tampere, she was the youngest child in a family of five children. Her father was a carpenter, and her mother did odd jobs around town, mostly catering.

I remember we lived on a big rock, and we kids did a lot of running around on the rocks. I had a very good childhood in many ways and I can say that my life was pretty good. Our home had two rooms: a kitchen with a pretty big oven, it took a lot of space, and one bedroom. There were five of us children running around. We did not have our own rooms, but we did well. We had sheep and one goat at one point as well, I think.

Her most vivid memory from childhood, she says, is from when she was 10:

I was waiting for my father to come home and they called and said that he was injured, that we should come to have a look. My mother went to see him and I waited at home. And what happened was he was brought back home in a coffin.

That memory will never fade.

By this time, all her older siblings had already left home, so Saima and her mother lived alone for the next few years, until Saima was 14, when she took a job as a nanny in Tampere. Three years later, in 1930, when she was 17, she made the move to factory life.

I went to Tampella clothes factory and asked for a job. They said they had just one open position, in the sewing shop. And so I started trying to convince them that I was good in handcrafts. I said that I had the best grade in handcrafts at school. Then the doorkeeper told the sewing master to come downstairs and I started working there – it was my first factory job.

I worked there for three and half years. We sewed tarps for the state and sacks for flavorings. Everything was packaged in sacks back then. We also did bed linens and towels and finer textile work. I worked in every department.

Then I switched to a job at the Tricot factory in Pyynikki [a Tampere district]. I was fighting with management about my salary. We were all fighting about our salaries.

---

* In the pre-hospital era, as was the case with its Russian counterpart, the banya, the family or village sauna was the most hygienic place to give birth.

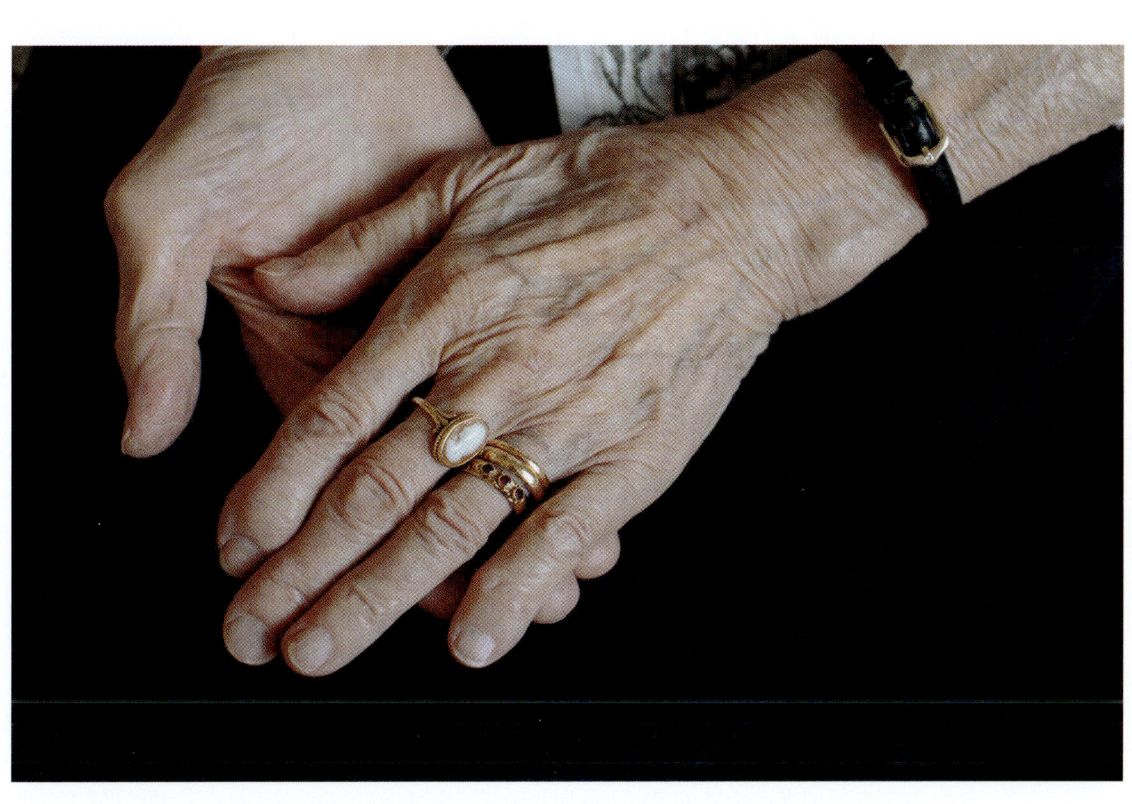

All the girls said that, if we didn't get a pay increase, we would leave. But when the moment came to leave, I was the only one who actually left.

I left and the others stayed. But I was lucky. The next day I went to the gate of the Tricot factory and I got a job that same day for 50 pennies more in salary than where I had come from. The other girls were a bit sour, because they did not come with me. But I got lucky.

I have always been determined. If I decide that I will do this or that, I'm not going to retreat.

Saima clearly found a kindred soul in her husband, Mauno Johannes Ritahlahti. He was five years older, and they met in 1936, when she was 21.

At that time in Tampere, there was a place owned by the worker's union – a summer cottage. That is where I met my husband. He visited that place and so did I. That is where it began, and we were together 30 years.

I have always been determined. If I decide that I will do this or that, I'm not going to retreat.

The couple planned to be married on November 1, 1941, but Finland was mobilizing for WWII, which in Finland is called The Continuation War, because it followed so closely on the heels of the Winter War between Finland and the USSR.

My husband was working in Jalasjärvi then, and he was supposed to come to our wedding, but he did not want to take public transport, because the general mobilization for the war had been started [and he could have been forcibly taken off to join the army]. So he got a bicycle and rode it from Jalasjärvi to Tampere, 160 kilometers, to get married. We got married, and after that he signed up for the army.

During the war, Mauno worked as a driver in the military, driving German officers around.* Meanwhile, Saima continued working in Tampere but did not live in the city, which, as an industrial center, was heavily bombed by Allied planes.

I escaped the war to Ylöjärvi, so I did not have to hide from the bombings at night. I was with my old mother, or when you think about it now, she was not that old. I came [to Tampere] by bus and went back in the evening... I was pretty safe there in the countryside. The war did not have so big an impact on me, although it did for my husband, sister's husband, and many others… In the countryside, you did not see so much of the war. You had food and something to drink... I sent many packages of butter to my sister in Tampere. She sent me an empty ration card, and I sent back butter. That was life during the emergency period: everything had to be bought on ration cards.

* Finland allied with Nazi Germany in 1941.

Finnish still life with flowers.

Saima's family tree.

Finland capitulated and negotiated a peace with the Soviet Union in late 1944, one of the terms of which was to remove Germans from all of Finnish territory, mainly in areas of Lapland – the far North, which Germany valued particularly for its nickel mines. Mauno shifted from driving around Germans to driving around Russians, who were verifying that the Germans had indeed left. He was trusted because he could not understand Russian.

The Germans, for their part, practiced a scorched earth policy, decimating towns throughout northern Finland as they retreated. An estimated 100,000 Finns lost their homes.

One of the scorched northern towns was Rovaniemi, which is where Mauno and Saimi moved after the war was over, to rebuild and run a textile plant.

Saima and Mauno had three children, born in 1942, 1945, and 1947. The eldest, son Tapani, moved to the US, where he died in the early 1990s. Their middle child, a daughter Sirkka, moved to Sweden when she was 18 and lives there to this day. The youngest daughter, Eila, stayed in Finland. Between them all, Saima now has nine grandchildren and eight great-grandchildren.

In her century of life, Saima has traveled rather a lot: to the US and southern Europe, and even to the USSR, but she says she cannot remember any of the trips – these memories seem to have faded. Of the changes she has seen in Finland, she is terse, and neither philosophical nor judgemental.

There have been a lot, of course. Before, it was much poorer. Everything is better now.

Looking back over the century, she is generally happy with her life.

I had a good marriage. I had a good husband, I have no complaints about him. He took care of me... I did not have too many hard times. I did not have too many setbacks. But, of course, it was hard when I lost family members. Of course, I also had hard times, but I have forgotten them already...

While she may not look it, she says she very much feels like she is 100, because she is so clumsy and unable to remember as much as she would like. Plus, because she must eat through a feeding tube.

Life is normal, nothing special. The days are pretty similar... I have always done sport and even today try to stay in motion. The family takes me out for walks so that I am not stuck inside.

A nurse also comes to visit her every morning and evening, to help with her feeding tube and medicines. She keeps active with handicrafts and a bit of reading. Yet she rues not being able to go to dance clubs anymore.

It kept my mind young.

She credits her longevity to her high level of activity and says she would advise youth who want to live out a century to simply:

Live a normal life: no smoking and no hard booze.

When asked about her thoughts about Russia or the Soviet Union, she offers a very relaxed view of the nation with which Finland has had a very complicated history during her lifetime.

I never thought of it as any different than other countries. People there are the same as here. Some say that Russians are Russians, but I always thought they are the same as we are. They sometimes had different sorts of leaders than we did, and that style would not have suited us, perhaps. But with people, there is no difference. Leaders are different, but people are the same everywhere.

LYUBOV IVANOVNA PAKHOMOVA
POKROVKA VILLAGE, NOVOSIBIRSK OBLAST
2 AUGUST 1917

To get to the village of Pokrovka from Novosibirsk requires a 250-kilometer, four-hour drive over gut-pounding roads. The broken, humpy asphalt trails through wide, open fields of knee-high wheat (it grows shorter here) that are broken by lines and copses of birch and capped with tremendous cloud structures left behind by the previous day's storm. Numerous raptors are sighted circling the fertile, rodent-filled fields, or perching atop telephone poles or rolls of hay.

The village – just a stone's throw from the border with Altai Krai, was once part of a thriving kolkhoz. But now it is empty, save for three families. An abandoned village store, topped by a rusting satellite dish, sits on the edge of an overgrown field. At the other end of the field, bordering a horse paddock, is a slowly crumbling monument to those who fell in World War II.

Opposite the shuttered store is the only home in the village that shows any evidence of life. And here it is in abundance. A hand-painted sign warns of dogs behind the fence, and there are three, all of them chained up. One is a shaggy dog about half the size of the dozen broiler chickens roaming the yard; the second is a puffy, squeaking puppy full of rambunctious energy; the third is a large German Shepherd who sounds fierce but is, in fact, a marshmallow that would just love to crawl into your lap.

The log and plank outbuildings (shed, banya, outhouse) are run-down but solid. Between the garden and the home's front door is an overstuffed chair infested with kittens.

The house itself is small but solidly built. It was erected long ago for a school director, and it has the inviting feeling of a home where every corner is put to use, combined with the awkwardness of a century-old design that is somewhat inappropriate for modern living.

Lyubov Pakhomova, fully blind and nearly deaf, sits on a couch at one end of the large family room, clearly anticipating visitors.

"Some guests are here to see you," Lyubov's granddaughter-in-law Irina announces.

"Have you come for me?" Lyubov replies.

Irina smiles, patient and reassuring, "No, no, babushka, No one is taking you anywhere. They are guests."

Before Lyubov moved in with Irina and her husband Nikolai, she was living in a neighboring district with her daughter. When the daughter passed away, Lyubov said to Irina and Nikolai, "Take me to an old folks' home, you don't need to be worrying about me." The couple scoffed at the idea and scolded Lyubov for even thinking such a thing. And they brought her back to Pokrovka, to live with them and their teenage daughter, Alexandra, in the village where Lyubov had lived most of her life.

Mama had many children – 12, but only six lived to grow up. I had a brother born in '05, a sister in '08, me in '17, a brother after me in '20, another in '22, and the last brother in '29... We lived in Kaluzhskaya, which was a gubernia then...We were poor. The land was bad, loamy, the crops were bad. So, nothing to brag about.

*We moved to Siberia in the 20s... Lenin gave the land, so whoever wanted to could voluntarily resettle in wild Siberia...**

We lived in Volchno-Burla for two years. They gave us a village so a land surveyor would show up and measure out plots for everyone. And then we moved to Pokrovka...

Our parents built a hut, and our family lived there. It was just a log hut with a grass roof that first summer. We worked like peasants, sowing, plowing, harvesting. I went to school in 192–... Oh, wait, what year was that? I was 10 or 11. And I went to school. They opened a school here...

---

* In 1920, a serious drought, exacerbated by mindless, ideologically-driven government policies, led to a horrific famine across Russia's and Ukraine's agricultural regions. By early 1921, Soviet power, fighting the final battles of the Civil War, was faced with massive peasant uprisings, largely as a result of the state's expropriation of all agricultural output. The introduction of NEP (the New Economic Policy) in March of 1921 reversed government policy on agriculture and trade, and gave farmers increased freedoms and incentives to produce. As a result, by the mid-1920s, Siberia had become one of the most important agricultural regions in Russia.

The wide Siberian plain west of Novosibirsk.

Go to school they said. But what school? It was a sort of a collective, they called it. A collective collected there. In some sort of house... It was packed, everyone had lots of kids then... But everyone was eager to go to school.

I was born in '17, but there were kids older than me going to school... then they sent us a young teacher, and the teenagers started harrassing her. So someone came from the regional leadership and they kicked the older kids out, but they left the younger ones who were better suited for school...

*We sat four to a school desk... and back then we dressed in what we could, in what we made ourselves. Some shirt or other, a blouse, a skirt. Those were our clothes. As for shoes, some had them, others wore lapti. I wore lapti.**

Times were hard, but the family was better off in Siberia than they had been in the West. Until, that is, Collectivization arrived.

When we moved here, we were sowing by ourselves, plowing and harvesting on our own. There was bread to our heart's content. The hunger, it was gone. In Siberia we didn't have hunger. It was only when we lived in Kaluga Gubernia that we went hungry. We never ate pure bread. We added chaff or other things to it. But in Siberia we ate white bread...

The kolkhozes came in the 30s. It arrived here in '30. Before that, we lived on our own, kept a bit of cattle. Sheep, cows, calves, horses – it was all our own...

There was a general meeting, where they explained the rules of the kolkhoz. And then they signed people up. How they signed people up, I don't know, I can't say. Some wanted to, some didn't. Those who didn't, they became kulaks... Those who feared dekulakization† *likely signed up for the kolkhoz.*

Her family was divided on whether or not to join.

Father spoke with Mother. Mother didn't want to. I know that the women got together and broke up the meeting. They didn't want to join the kolkhoz. Ours too. The men said that it could not be avoided, that they recommended we join. Father signed up. Those who were a bit richer, or more upstanding, they were sent off somewhere. Labeled as kulaks or fools, the devil knows what...

We had to give the kolkhoz four horses – three were workhorses, and there were two young foals. Then we had to give a calf or a cow. They were creating a general kolkhoz herd.

By joining the kolkhoz, the family was agreeing, reluctantly, to tie its future to the future of the farm. If it did well, they would be paid in kind, if not, they would have to make do with less. It was a radical reform of agriculture that was

---

* Shoes woven from birch bark strips (bast).

† See footnote, page page 92.

central to Stalin's theory of rapid industrialization for the Soviet Union. And it would prove as disastrous as it was cruel and oppressive.

People fled. How could you live?... Some fled to Leningrad, others elsewhere. Through the river ports. They ran off to cut peat, to earn a bit. And then those people, they could not get passports. And then people demanded their passports, so they all had to return. Without a passport you can't live, can't get set up anywhere...

In 1941, Lyubov and two friends had reached a breaking point.

There was nothing here, nothing to eat, nothing to wear, nothing to put on your feet. And our Kaluga relatives, they had children, and they worked in peat operations. So we sent them a letter. And they proposed to us: come here, join our kolkhoz...

They planned to escape at night, and it was no small undertaking.

We finished work. I worked as a milkmaid. The other person worked as a bookkeeper at the farm. And the third worked as a groom. We decided, let's run off, maybe we can get in at the peat operations – there they were earning 80-90 rubles a month, that's what they wrote us. So we finished our workday and we decided to flee at night so that no one could stop us...

We finished our workday and we decided to flee at night so that no one could stop us...

And so at night we walked 20 kilometers to the village of Reshyoty... There, we found some kolkhozniks who were driving to Kargat for fuel, and we paid one of them and he took us. And in Kargat we got tickets to Belev station in Kaluga Oblast.

It took fully two weeks to travel the 3300 kilometers by train to Belev, and to this day, Lyubov readily recalls the dates of her travel.

We left March 24 and on April 7 arrived in Yaroslavl Oblast... And they didn't catch us on the road [for traveling without a passport]. When we arrived there they gave us a six-month passport.

How did they survive the long journey? What did they bring with them?

We took some stuff with us. We took dried bread crusts – they were sour, the flour had wormwood in it... that's how we went and what we ate. Nothing worth noting down...

We took a change of clothes, a shirt, and a skirt.

Once they had arrived, the young women were given a modest advance, boarded in a barracks and put to work.

We dried peat. We formed it, dried it, put it in stacks so that it would dry out. There was all sorts of work. Shifting it around on pallets. Hard, that work was.

And they got paid the promised 98 rubles a month, but there was nothing extra to send back to Pokrovka, to her parents, brothers, and a daughter born in 1935. Plus, the work only lasted a few months, because two months after they arrived, the Germans attacked.

This is how we found out. We got up early, at 4, in order to get to work by 8. We got up, and there was a radio apparatus hanging there. It squawked, then stopped, then

Opposite page, an afternoon feast that included chicken "that had been pecking in the yard this morning," and a cat-infested easy chair. Below, Lyubov takes an afternoon nap.

squawked, then stopped again. But we gathered around, some were joking, some were putting on their shoes, others getting dressed. And suddenly they declared that it was war. That Hitler was already bombing us.

Oy, how I had forgotten that, Lord! I tell you honestly, I had forgotten that... Kiev! They had already bombed Kiev, and they declared that it had started. June 22, exactly at 4 am, they bombed Kiev, and they declared to us that war had begun. You understand?

And yet, they had to go to work that day.

How else? But what sort of work? We hardly worked all day. Just listened. Molotov spoke. He called on all workers, all peasants, that they not let us be defeated. We... well it was like that all day. We'd work a bit, then listen to the radio. And our life flowed on. Immediately there were rations... Rations for everyone...

She worked at the peat operation until September. Since it was so close to Moscow, she and her co-workers were all evacuated, and so she returned home to Siberia, not even working a full season. For three days their train stood on a siding in Moscow, and then it traveled slowly back toward Novosibirsk.

What was the country saying? Well, they were evacuating people from around Moscow. Everyone was going somewhere, to Tashkent or wherever. Where they were headed, I don't know. Some said things. Some said that they would not take our country. Others said that there would be chaos.

What did I think? I was awfully scared. Day and night I prayed that the hated serpent would not get to Moscow.

After returning to Pokrovka and the collective farm, life was no better – worse in fact – than when she had fled a few months before.

Everything, they said, for the front. Everything for the front. And people did not resist. Everything for the front so that we can be liberated...

We knitted mittens, socks. Sewed handkerchiefs, put them in parcels. Everyone helped out...

In 1943 she met and married her husband Nikolai, who was 18 years older than her.

His wife died in '43 and he was alone. And I didn't have anywhere to go. In '42. And, well, we were acquainted and got married.

Of course, there was no real wedding.

There was nothing to eat, but we did do some celebrating.

When the war was over, all of Lyubov's brothers returned; only one had been seriously wounded – his arm no longer functioned.

Victory day. We were digging in the garden. There was nothing to plow with, so we did it with our hands, digging. We had eaten some lunch, and I had two girls then. One

Lyubov's parents and her brother Pyotr's family.

The family's backyard.

Lyubov with her granddaughter-in-law Irina and great-granddaugther Alexandra.

born in '35, the other in '43. I had to go to work and was waiting for my niece Manya, who was coming to babysit my littlest girl.

I am waiting, looking, and for a long time nothing.

"Manya, why did you take so long?"

And she says, "Auntie, the war is over."

And I say, "Who told you that?"

"It's over, auntie," she smiles. "They fed us lunch, gave us each a piece of bread with soup. And they said that the war was over."

Oh, Lord! I look and see what is going on outside: some are waving their arms about, some are crying, and so on. So many had been killed.

We ran to each other, hugged and kissed. Everyone was happy...

That night, no one slept. We ran to visit one another, shared tears.

Then later we started to find out who returned alive... in some families, two or three had been killed. We had a family, Darya Ledankova, her husband was killed... her son disappeared, and she received the death certificate for her other son. Three… Another family, the father was killed and two sons. And others lost just one. That's how it was...

Things didn't get better immediately after the war.

There were shortages, hunger... Everyone suffered, but no one grumbled. You had to give them eggs, give them meat…

The family had tough times. There was a brief move out to the Rostov-on Don region, ostensibly to help keep the family of one of her daughters (Nikolai's mother) together. But it did not work, the couple divorced, and the parents and daughter, together with Lyubov's grandchildren, returned to Pokrovka. Nikolai recalls a rather trying childhood.

He remembers his grandfather as a sharp, difficult man who often beat him. And this cruelty may have contributed to his end. Irina shares how the daughters from her grandfather's first marriage moved him into an old folk's home as part of a plot to manipulate his home out from under him, to get his money.

I don't know. I didn't do anything special. I lived like everyone else.

On the other hand, Nikolai remembers his grandmother Lyuba as "the mountain" to which they all felt anchored, the rock of the family. "She never swore. She was always a very calm woman," he says.

In her youth, Irina adds, Lyubov was told by a gypsy woman that she would live a long life, but also, that there would be grief in her life.

Which makes one wonder, why does Lyubov feel she has lived to be 100?

I don't know. I didn't do anything special. I lived like everyone else. And even had more of the bad. And almost none of the good...

I got sick often, got diagnosed with a nervous heart. Then, I don't know. You think that I lived easily? Oh, my dear, there was everything: both hunger and cold, a lack of both shoes and clothing. I don't know why I lived so long. Perhaps one just has to work more and lie down less.

Is there anything else she would like out of this life?

What then? Oh, I don't know. To die, have a funeral, and be buried.

But not to live any longer?

To live? Yes, well, everyone wants to live. I'm living. But I need to be taken care of. Ira here, she works; Kolya also is very busy with things. And then I have to be cared for. It's time to die, to be set aside.

GALINA VALERYANOVNA GREBNEVA
MOSCOW
19 AUGUST 1917

Galina Grebneva (born Kortova) is a diminutive woman with straight hair cut just below her chin line. Completely blind and with slightly diminished hearing, she is a profoundly tender soul. She smiles and laughs when complimented on how nice she looks in a special yellow dress. It is the same one she wore 60 years ago to the coronation of Queen Elizabeth.

When guided, she moves around her apartment with relative ease, scarcely admitting to being tired, even though she must rest halfway between the living room and kitchen. When asked how she is doing, she replies with a sing-song, legato-cadenced "*kha-ra-sho*" ("fine"). When asked what is her favorite meal, she replies without hesitation, "Caviar on *buterbrody*" (an open-faced sandwich). She has a sweet tooth and repeatedly asks for just a bit more sugar in her tea.

Galina lives with her daughter Irina in a cozy two-room apartment, one room of which is a museum to Galina's life, filled with displays of photographs, awards, and timelines arranged for the groups of students that regularly stop by to visit and hear her 70- and 80-year-old stories. A handwritten family tree stretches across the table. Compiled a decade ago, it is kept up to date with penciled inscriptions – the newest members struggle to remain on the page.

Irina is a whirling dervish of energy. She imposes a strict daily routine on her mother's life, keeping her active and lovingly peppering her with suggestions: "Mama, stand up straight... Deep breaths... Lift your legs higher as you walk..."

"She is a child," Irina confides later. "What do you expect? I sleep with her... She can no longer dress herself or get up on her own." And just two weeks before she almost lost her life. She rode in an ambulance for the first time ever, in

order to be treated for a severe, life-threatening case of bronchitis. It took a great measure of pushiness and work for Irina to get the doctors at the hospital to care about her 100-year-old mother, to put her on antibiotics and treat her raging fever. Even protestations that Galina was a war veteran and blockade survivor fell on deaf ears.

For all that, Galina is imperturbable (and her cough is largely gone). Her blindness causes her to aim her gaze higher than normal, and she occasionally flicks back her hair and twitches her head as she talks, as if self-conscious of the camera she cannot see. Her voice is clear and musical, occasionally jumping half an octave on softer vowels. At times her replies to questions seem a bit rehearsed, as if she is delivering them to a class of Young Pioneers. Yet she is always very precise and concise.

Her life began in Samara, on August 19, 1917.

About my parents... My father, Valerian Ivanovich, had a wonderful voice. He sang in the Mariinsky Theater. A superb tenor. And Mama, she was a kindergarten teacher.

But it turned out for me that my parents separated early and left me with my grandmother, in Samara. So I swam in the Volga, bathed there... I have very fond memories of my childhood.

When it came time to start school, Galina and her mother and grandmother moved to Leningrad.

It was very difficult for me. I was in kindergarten and had to walk alone to school through Mars Field... along Nevsky Prospekt.

Indeed, repeated queries about Galina's childhood brings up only this memory of her earliest days in the city.

After high school, she entered the Institute of Railway Transport, training to be an electrical engineer.

In 1937, while still a student, Galina met her future husband, Sergei.

He was three years older than me. I was in the first year, he was already in the third. He led our classes. As he would say, he saw me when he first walked into the classroom and immediately fell in love. I sort of gradually fell in love with him. For him, it was at first glance.

After classes, he would accompany me home. Sergei and I sang in a choir together; the choir brought us together.

Sergei did so well at the institute that he was selected to study at the Higher Party School, which Stalin had set up in 1939 to train the best and brightest cadres. The couple would not marry until 1945, carrying out a tender correspondence during the war that has been preserved and bound in the family archive.

Galina as a young child.

Galina, with her husband Sergei.

I got excellent marks all five years. I finished up during the blockade, * *but classes were being held during the bombardment, the ceaseless bombardment. Every day I walked to classes. A rocket never fell on me.*

Of course, we went hungry, because they only gave us, I forget, I think it was 125 grams of bread.

Despite being a natural leader and a strong student, Galina was not initially allowed into the Komsomol, because of her family's "noble status" – her mother's grandfather, Kapiton Ivanov, was a peasant who had gained noble status for his service in the Crimean War (1853-56).

Yet she persisted. During the war, Irina recalls, Sergei wrote to Galina, saying, "Galochka, I would like for you to join the party. Do you need my recommendation?" During the difficult first year of the blockade, she was finally allowed into the Komsomol, and then, when she graduated, into the Party.

They looked at me, Lord, you could see my ribs... I was a skeleton. The women cried.

Soon thereafter, in 1942, when a chance came to be evacuated from Leningrad, Galina was told that only one person could accompany her.

We had to leave grandma behind. She died because she could not even go out to get bread. But I took Mama with me.

Papa was living in Kirov at that time. I arrived in Kirov and my father's new wife took care of me for two weeks. I could not even raise my arms, I was so weak.

I was taken by a neighbor to a banya there. And of course I had not undressed for several months, and when I did, the women there all began to cry. They looked at me, Lord, you could see my ribs, and instead of a stomach there was a pit, and sticks for legs with circles for knees. I was a skeleton. The women cried.

During the war, Galina worked on the railroad in Omsk, and Sergei fought "on four fronts." After the war was over, in September 1945, Galina and Sergei were married and Sergei entered the diplomatic service.

The couple's first diplomatic posting was to South Africa (1947-49), followed by England (1952-54),† Ceylon (1957-59), Batumi (1964-68), and finally Spitsbergen (1972-76).

While in England, Galina taught kindergarten, set up a children's choir, and attended the coronation of Queen Elizabeth.

The American children's choir had been in first place. But after we arrived, we took first place...

I worked in the kindergarten, and there was a park next to the embassy. After lunch we would go to the park to practice our singing and dancing... all the dances, all the songs were taught outdoors...

---

* The Siege of Leningrad lasted from September 8, 1941, until January 27, 1944.

† Just one year after the Soviet-recruited spies Burgess and Maclean defected to the USSR.

She [Elizabeth] was, of course, a fine person... Each embassy had its designated place in the park, and she walked by and gave everyone [commemorative] medals from her coronation. She was such a lively person.

In 1967, while in Moscow between postings, Irina recalls, the family was given a *samizdat* copy of Aleksandr Solzhenitsyn's nove, *The First Circle.* They were only allowed to keep it for two days. Galina and Sergei read it simultaneously, "one passing a finished page to the next. They did not sleep for two nights," Irina says.

"Papa said that it could not be true, that he did not believe it [that there were forced labor groups in factories]... But Mama said that it actually might be true. She had seen, she had experienced how people could disappear. How these trucks drove around with 'Bread' or 'Produce' written on the sides. There was not so much produce in Moscow, and therefore they had to be hauling people around in them."

Irina underscores, however, that "we are a completely non-political family. For each, the most important thing is to work, to help, for those who can, to help." And her parents did not bring their work home, Irina says, for "everywhere there hung those slogans, 'the enemy is always listening,' The enemy. That's how it was. There was always some sort of enemy..."

After her father died, Irina says, she asked her mother if he had been involved with the KGB, as that was very common for long-serving diplomats. "She said that they tried to recruit him," Irina recalls, "even brought him in, but that he refused. He did not agree... In general, he wanted to be a teacher. He was very intelligent, Papa was. He was like our encyclopedia. He could answer any question. Absolutely anything."

He was a very good man. Very smart. We lived together as best friends. We sang in the choir together. Second, we both were skiers. Then we took up table tennis. So we had common interests.

The family was always close, always active in sports and outdoor activities together, and every Saturday they all cleaned the apartment together. They were never rich, and Irina notes how humbly they lived.

"When people came to visit, they could not believe that this was the apartment of a diplomat's family," Irina says. "Everything was very modest. We didn't spend money on anything... but we always went to the theater... we, the whole family together, went to the Moscow swimming pool, which is now the Cathedral of Christ the Savior. Different things were valuable to us, you see?"

Galina never raised her voice to her children, Irina says. In fact, when she was angry, she would go completely silent. "Maybe she just didn't know how to get angry, that her character was just like that. Better to be silent... Then we

Galina wearing the yellow dress she wore to Queen Elizabeth's Coronation in June 1953 (left, in London with her husband and other diplomats).

One of the apartment's rooms has been transformed into a living museum of Galina's life, to be shared with visiting students and journalists.

Daughter Irina offers Galina her favorite treat: buterbrody with caviar.

children would all be in a hurry to apologize." Their father, the diplomat, was the one with a temper, Irina says. "He could explode. But it would quickly pass."

Even today, two of Galina's children call her every night to check up on her. Once a month, on special days, a cousin comes and takes Galina and Irina to a church three minutes away – Peter and Fevronia Church. Galina and Sergei embraced the Church in the 1990s, after the Soviet system fell. And in 1999, a few years before Sergei died, the couple had an official church wedding.

When asked how one lives to be 100, Galina is characteristically terse:

Do sports. Do something interesting. Make life good in your family.

What is the secret to long life? You must help people.

Galina is sitting at the table in the kitchen and asks for a bit more to eat.

"And what can I give your highness?" Irina asks in a love-laced reference to the family's distant, noble past.

"Well, perhaps some caviar *buterbrody*?"

YELIZAVETA ANDREYEVNA LAKEYEVA
KONEVO, NIZHNY NOVGOROD OBLAST
1 SEPTEMBER 1917

The village of Konevo, Nizhny Novgorod Oblast, is in the sticks.

But in a good way.

The villagers live in homes decorated with carved window-surrounds, but without fences. Aside from electricity, civilization has not set foot here. There is not even a local store.

But there are birds flitting about, bees buzzing, winds whispering through the forest, and a small, burbling brook. It is a marvelous village. One dreams of being born here, living out one's life, having ten children and an unfathomable number of grandchildren, then dying happy and satisfied in one's old age.

For this reason, this place is highly prized by dacha dwellers, and so they comprise the plurality of residents here in summer. But in the winter the village is suffocated by high snow drifts and darkness – only endured by three permanent residents. One of them is the locally famous Yelizaveta Lakeyeva.

Yelizaveta is an adroit old woman. She moves about her large, timeworn home and garden without a walking stick or any other form of support. She is entirely independent, bustling about her property and working with great zeal. She even does her own shopping: a few times a week a mobile store visits the village and stops near her home. A long line of neighbors forms to buy various staple items, but they let her jump to the head of the queue; some will also help her carry her bags of produce back home.

Most of what Yelizaveta cooks is rather simple, yet she still bakes pies in her wood-burning stove. Most surprisingly, in the winter she stokes the stove herself – it's one of those massive pieces of masonry that sits in the middle of the *izba*. In the summer, she is busy in the garden – opening the greenhouse in the morning, closing it up in the evening, and watering her plants in between.

Strictly speaking, Yelizaveta is alone. She was married twice, and both times it turned out well. Except that she never had any children, and her second husband died long ago. Yet she still has a large family and a wide circle of friends.

First of all, everyone in the village knows everyone else. Unlike in cities, where there is a measure of personal space, here the borders between individuals are all but washed away. There is always someone with whom one can discuss the uncomplicated rural news. For example, Yelizaveta has a 95-year-old friend who lives in the next house. They grew up together, which means they always have something to reminisce about.

Second, a social worker, Valentina, comes to visit Yelizaveta several times a week to clean up around the house, prepare some meals, and just chat. Valentina is a nice, open-hearted person, and she and Yelizaveta have formed such a close bond that they could easily be mistaken for family members.

Third, Yelizaveta has a niece, Alexandra – a calm, hard-working, seldom-smiling, and rarely-speaking woman. Alexandra lives in the nearby city, but spends the summer with her aunt, and comes to visit her weekly in the winter. Alexandra takes care of Yelizaveta's old home; it would be very difficult for Yelizaveta to cope without her.

I was born in Konevo. My parents farmed. They had lots of livestock: cows and horses, and all sorts. Mother and Father had a farm. We were eight children that survived. Three died.

When I was born, Father was in the war, in the revolution. I remember my father... I was maybe four. He always called me, "Nanny-goat, nanny-goat, nanny-goat!" My father joked around with me. I remember that and will never forget it.

She also remembers how her father, Andrei, told her stories about the taking of Port Arthur. In her memory, it is some sort of important building, and if her father said "took it," then that means they won.

Based on this scrap of information, one can presume that in 1904 her father took part in the Russo-Japanese War, in the defense of the Russian naval base at Port Arthur, China. After a long siege, the Russian fortress was eventually lost.

Her father is also connected with another very clear memory:

We went to school. The teacher, well, we had celebrations. Not really celebrations, just assemblies for the children. The parents would come, they'd start off with The Internationale. *All the men, all the fathers. And our father was there. They stood there and we watched. They sang this song, that anthem thing. Oh, how did it go?*

Yelizaveta still does her own shopping and cooking. A few times a week a mobile store visits the village and stops near her home (above). Below, her modest kitchen.

Yelizaveta is an adroit old woman. She bustles about her large, timeworn home and garden, working with considerable zeal.

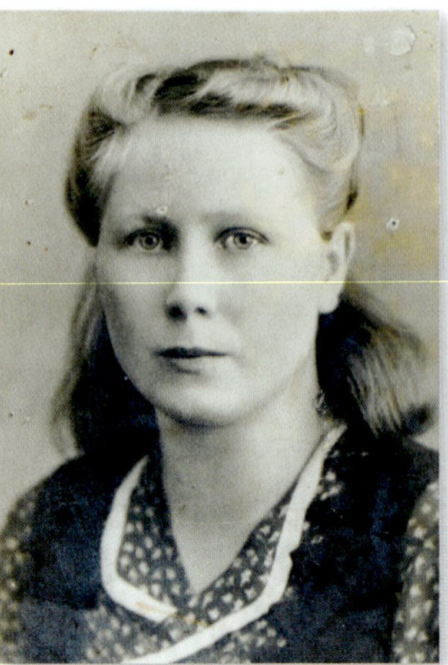

Yelizaveta today, and as a young woman.

With her sisters. Yelizaveta is in the white dress.

Arise, all victims of oppression,
Earth's hungry, caught in slavery's thrall.
We will achieve our liberation.
Those who were nothing will be all.

And I looked and Father started singing this song. Everyone was singing. That was after the coup. That was probably after Collectivization. So the children were at their desks, and the parents were standing, singing together. And we sang along.

Yelizaveta also recalls with a laugh how she and other children pestered the village priest. They would pluck the berries from his raspberry plants that stuck through his fence. And they would gather up potato fruits* and toss them onto the tin roof of the priest's house: "boom, boom, boom!" He would run outside, cursing the children and their mother, Agrippina.

Mother didn't like priests.

She also remembers well how in the 1930s priests and monks were repressed, how church property was stolen.

Yes, they closed [the church] and looted it. They took away the bells, took the icons from the village. They took everything away. It was the local authorities, the village soviet I think.

But what was interesting, was when the deacon took down the bell. He was standing on the crossbeam, they had hung the bell on a log. And he was sawing the log, so the bell would fall. "You're gonna go flying too," someone says. "You're standing on the same log." How they laughed at that deacon! Why was he working so hard? So they wouldn't exile him. After all, lots of priests were sent into exile. It was very cold then. Sent them somewhere in the North, I don't know where. Many died...

The windowless, decapitated church still stands at the edge of the village. It was never fully demolished. Inside, trees took root, and there is a thick beam, stuck into the ground and decayed by time. On the façade of the church, on both sides of the entrance, are two empty stone niches, each about the height of a human being. In them, at approximately the height where a face might be, there are chinks that appear to have been carved out by bullets. Likely someone shot at the church, aiming at the eyes in saints' frescoes that were mounted in the niches.

The repressions did not touch Yelizaveta's family. They got off with just losing some of their property to the kolkhoz: a horse, one of their two cows, sleds, their barn, and granary. But it became a doubly offensive act when their confis-

* A hard, green fruit that grows from the top of the potato plant. It looks like a cherry tomato, but is inedible.

cated property was allowed to rot – a vivid illustration of the sad but true saying, that "everyone's is no one's."

Then the kolkhoz was set up, and after that blow, we started to live a bit better. But we worked in the kolkhoz then.

Only, instead of receiving a wage, they received "empty sticks" ("*palki*"): for each day of a kolkhoz worker's labor.* Then, when it came time to gather the harvest, they would receive, for example, a kilogram of grain for each "stick." Or they would receive nothing if the harvest was poor.

At 16, Yelizaveta left the kolkhoz. They let her go. She got a job in the neighboring town as a nurse and took classes in order to become a preschool director. When she had free time she returned to Konevo to help her parents earn money. She helped her father make harness shafts for carts, and charcoal – all to sell. With her mother, she collected pinesap in the forest to be made into turpentine and rosin – again, selling it for cash. And this is how they lived until June of 1941.

We were out having a good time. The war began at exactly four in the morning. We all ran home from our celebrating, to our separate apartments. But cars overtook us: they came from the regional committee to gather up all the young men. It was dawn, but the guys were out walking with their accordion, some sobbing, some dancing.

In the first days of the war, Yelizaveta worked in the village council, helping draw up draft orders for the front. Then she was put in charge of two preschools.

There were lots of children at that time. They were brought from Moscow, Brest, Mogilev – from various cities. They were evacuees, not locals. All the children were brought to me, but their mothers worked in the kolkhoz.

Then, two years later, her profession changed radically:

I got a job in a military defense unit of the river fleet, as a sharpshooter. There were no more men, and we young women were put to work. They taught us to face left and right and how to belly-crawl. We studied weapons and defended things of value. And it was very dangerous, scary. Anything suspicious we reported to the guardhouse. But some made attempts. They were walking suspiciously along the Volga, with cords, wanting to blow up our station. We informed on them. They were checked out, picked up and sent somewhere. Nobody told us anything. Germans, probably. It was very dangerous work.

Yelizaveta also had to guard and accompany arrestees. She recalls being a sensitive woman with a large gun, and how she led a group of men from the guardhouse to dinner, saying to them, "Boys, don't run away from me. I got a

---

* See discussion, page 112

A wooden bridge leads to Yelizaveta's home.
A teapot waits in an aperture of the home's large Russian stove.

boss watching over me, and if you run off, it will turn out bad for me." Once she even had to lead her own sister behind the barrel of a gun. She had been arrested because, while working on a fire brigade, she was unable to put out a fire in a store that burned down. Her sister got lucky: she was let go.

Work as a guard was not so bad, as wartime jobs went. They got a daily ration of 800 grams of bread. They were even fed meat, because the security guards started a farm that kept cows and pigs. The girls were sated and even found time and energy to organize dances after work.

Then the war came to a close and with it Yelizaveta's youth.

Yes, I was happy. We relaxed in the evenings, enjoyed ourselves. But after the war there were no men, there was no one to marry. All of them came back wounded.

The war was a demographic tragedy for the country. All the men had been mercilessly mowed down.

But Yelizaveta did not stay single. She found a husband, and her spouse was a good, handsome, intelligent man, though he did suffer from lung disease.

Her mother-in-law insisted that the young bride not have any children, as she considered them a burden for a family in which the husband was not well. Yelizaveta agreed and thus did not become a mother. Today some say that's why she's lived to be 100 – she didn't have to worry herself sick about anyone.

After being widowed and living for a time alone, Yelizaveta once again found love and a partner. She was in her late 60s at the time and he was five years younger. She knew him well, as he was also from Konevo, and she agreed to marry, despite the fact that he wasn't the only one who sought her hand and heart. She smiles, remembering her decision: "I married a younger man, thinking that he would bury me. But no, I buried him."

So, already well on in years, Yelizaveta returned to her native Konevo from the regional center where she had been living. She didn't like her city apartment – it was cold, and the radiators fed by central heating never coped as well with the weather as does a Russian stove. Plus one does not feel as independent living in a concrete box as one does in a free-standing wooden home.

She does not complain about her age or her health. She plans to get her eyes fixed and go on living. But in her monologue, which is largely optimistic and life-affirming, a sad tone does slip in. She recalls the last time she saw her mother alive in the very home where she now lives. She had come from the city to visit her.

Momma was 104, and she says, "I don't wanna die. But, you see, I've become boring." She says, "Liza, stay another night with me." And I say, "Momma, I'll come back soon. Just three days, and I'll be back." And then they called: she died... How sad...

Yelizaveta's mother.

The destroyed village church.

HELMI HELLMAN
TAMPERE, FINLAND
17 SEPTEMBER 1917

When you see someone in their 100th year, you are almost certain to be deceived by outward appearances. It is very difficult to look beyond the weakened body before you to see the healthy, hardy person they once were. And it is, of course, impossible to guess by just looking at a person what sort of life stories are hidden in their aging brain.

Helmi Hellman lives alone, halfway down a clean, well-lit hallway in a clean, well-lit home for the elderly, in a light and airy southern district of Tampere. Her small, third-floor studio apartment has a calming view through tall pines onto Lake Villiänsalmi, where anchored sailboats bob quietly in the bay.

The walls of her home hold framed memories: a red cabin that was her childhood home, Helmi as acrobat, a sister lost to Stalin's purges, oil paintings, her parents. An old doll rests in the corner of the sofa, near an illuminated globe and a VHS machine.

Helmi is a small, slightly plump woman confined to a wheelchair. She has big, rheumy eyes, wide cheekbones, and a chronic cough that debilitates her at a few points in the interview, as when she laughs while telling a story about learning to high jump, and winning the district championship in running, high jump and long jump.

There is a sense of anxiety and hesitancy to her responses. She does not revel in remembering the past, for there are plenty of painful memories there, and few happy ones. She considers her greatest achievement in life that she just kept going.

I did not get totally depressed, but found a will to live after I started to be active in my hobbies. It has been hard, but I have managed to keep myself somewhat stable.

She was born Helmi Lahtinen in Pispala, an isthmus on the north side of Tampere, the daughter of Ida and Oskari, in a home that her father had built.

We were eight children, but many of them died at early ages. One died in the Civil War, as did my father. So my mother was taking care of three children. We lacked many things. My dad was a carpenter and mother stayed at home. When she was younger, she had worked as a maid in Karkkila.*

My dad and eldest brother died in a prison camp when I was five months old. (My father was cooking food for the Red troops and was arrested. This was supposed to be a sin.) It caused a trauma that still haunts me...

I always told my mother that she should find a father for me. I never got anything, and other children got more things. I was mad at my mom that she did not find a new father for me...

I suffered a lot when I was a child. People made fun of me and called me a "Red Orphan." It labeled me in a way that I was no longer considered a human being...

When I went to the teacher's desk, the teacher would pinch me. I was too afraid to say anything. Everyone saw that the teacher hated me because I was a Red Orphan, but that was not my fault or anything that I could change...

We weren't allowed to speak when we came into class. If someone said something, their name was put on the wall. My name was always there, even though I never spoke. And then I had to stand in the corner as punishment. Once I had to stand there even after the others went home. And I was thinking, "Why am I standing here?" So I went home, but then I realized that, of course, they would notice that I'd gone. So I went back. We had school in two shifts. So, during the evening shift, I had to stand in the corner...

That was my childhood. At school it was awful, I was bullied, other children bullied me and the teacher hated me.

It left a trauma that made me think I was worthless. But, despite that, I recovered when I grew up and started to have many hobbies. I noticed that I could do things and that lifted my self-confidence.

---

* Finland's Civil War lasted from January-May of 1918, as the country grappled with independence from the Russian empire. The Reds and Social Democratic Party, largely based in the cities and with the support of workers, tried to take control of the country, supported by the Soviet Red Army. The White forces, with its strength in the North and among rural sections of society, and supported by Germany, resisted, and was ultimately victorious, but there were bloody reprisals on both sides. Tampere, which had been a Red stronghold, was the site of particularly brutal anti-leftist reprisals. Some 80,000 Reds were imprisoned in POW camps, where the conditions were horrific.

The wall in Helmi's apartment is full of memories.

Sports and the arts saved Helmi.

I will always remember the time when I was little and my mother had to go to work. A single lady in Lempäälä took care of me, but also she had to work. So I was alone when I was five, and when I was alone, I danced and sang...

Helmi started to work at 17, in the Aaltone Shoe Factory, binding shoelaces. The girls there would compete to see who was fastest. "I came in second," Helmi smiles.

She worked at the factory for 30 years. But it was the extra-curricular activities that sustained her.

After I joined Tarmo, they saw my talent and put me in a trainer's course. I was instructing other women athletes, running programs for them and we had sports shows.*

* A workers' sports club.

Helmi (left) and her acrobat partner, 1942.

Helmi's sister, who emigrated to Canada, then to the USSR.

Helmi's third-floor studio apartment has a calming view through tall pines onto Lake Villiänsalmi.

We did gymnastics and danced. Slavic dances were in fashion back then and I was planning them. I also taught gymnastics and sport shows

We had such a good team that we were asked to go on a tour at the front. Our group of eight toured around Äänisjärvi to entertain the soldiers...*

We were performing all over Finland. For example, in 1945, we were so popular that we had 111 shows. "The only acrobats in Finland," "The best acrobats in Finland," that's how they advertised us...

I was the star everywhere we went. I was told that I was the best. Of course, one remembers such things.

Did she have a lot of male admirers at the front?

Of course, they were chasing me, but it was in vain.

Her love life, as it turned out, was filled with heartbreak. In 1940, she was engaged to be married to Into Moeseo. He was fighting in the Winter War, which started with the Soviet invasion in September 1939 (when the Soviets also invaded Eastern Poland) and ended in March 1940.

He was tall, handsome, and really nice. He was also in the Pispala Tarmo Sports Club, in a leadership position. That's how we met.

We were engaged. He was wounded on March 11, and the war ended on the 13th. He died on the 14th...

I remember when Into was brought back and I looked into the coffin. Why did he have to die just when the war was about to end? It was sad, I remember that. I had a black veil over my face...

That was my second great war trauma.

Seven years later, Helmi met Antti Hellman.

It started when I was doing music, and we were performing in the same event. That's how we met. We were married in 1947. He died in 1980.

But she demurs when asked about her 33-year marriage.

One thing I can say: My husband was a narcissist, and when I had a hard time, a friend came into my life and helped me start my life over.

Helmi's sister Klara, meanwhile, became one of the many Finns who emigrated from Finland to North America in the teens and 1920s. Many were persons with "Red sympathies" who fled Finland after the Civil War and were then, later, lured to the "workers' paradise" of the Soviet Union in the 1930s (after the Great Depression hit the West), to help build the economy of the Karelian Republic. By some estimates, as many as 10,000 Finns took this path.

---

* The Finnish name for Lake Onega.

She was 20 years old when she moved to Canada. She was there for a while and got married. Then she moved to the Soviet Union, and I visited them at their home as a tourist. But then Klara's husband became a victim of Stalin's purges. Stalin killed all the decent people there.

Klara had a girl and a boy, then the boy moved to Finland. But he died soon after he returned. And his family stayed and lived in Kaukajärvi.

Why did they go to the USSR? They were recruiting a lot of people at that time. Many people [Finns] went from America because it was a hard time in America.

My sister and her husband were working for a pittance in America and from there many were recruited to the Soviet Union. They went in that wave.

They worked on a forestry farm and my husband and I visited them. They had a house there and things were not too bad.

Despite this painful personal history, Helmi does not bear a grudge toward Finland's big neighbor to the east, but she is also a bit confused by recent events.

I don't know what to think [about Russia] anymore, because everything is going in a strange direction. I know that they got freedom there, and then some people stole everything and became rich. I don't accept that, but what can I do?

Russians? I respect them for some reason. Every time there's sport on TV, I support the Russians.

She claimed not to have anything meaningful to say about how things have changed over the last century:

Of course, things change. I cannot follow technology anymore. What changed is that we have food now, and different reasons to hurry.

But when asked what is the secret to long life, she has a quick and ready answer.

Sports. I have done gymnastics my whole life. I have been operated on 24 times, always on some different body part. But I have survived. That's because of sports. I did gymnastics when I was young, and also after I retired. Then I was also teaching gymnastics.

To this day, I go to the gym four times a week.

In the corner of the small apartment is a compact electric piano. When asked if she still plays, Helmi without hesitation wheels herself over to the corner and confidently bangs out a cheerful tune that she composed.

About her life, she says, she has few regrets.

I don't think I did anything wrong. The opposite, in fact: I was too nice. That is my character, I have never been able to say no...

[Life] did not give me much. I don't know if I'm satisfied or not. It has battered me so much, but I have survived.

Klara's husband became a victim of Stalin's purges. Stalin killed all the decent people there.

SABIRYAN ZINNATOVICH ASFANDIYAROV

SAKHAYEVO VILLAGE, BASHKIRIA

20 SEPTEMBER 1917

It is a 50-kilometer drive from Ufa, capital of Bashkiria, to the tiny farming village of Sakhayevo, over well-paved roads through rolling farmland. In several places, wide sunflower fields stretch to an azure horizon. Every few kilometers there are pull-outs for cars, tempting travelers with shaded picnic tables.

A local journalist, Rashid, is behind the wheel, driving with a nervous recklessness. His presence is vital, as centenarian Sabiryan Asfandiyarov is not only completely deaf but reportedly speaks no Russian, only Tatar. Rashid will interpret on the fly between Russian and Tatar.

Sabiryan sits in a comfortable easy chair in one corner of the living room of the family's cozy, one-story brick home. He is dressed in a light blue dress shirt, his bald head covered by a green Central Asian skullcap. His medal-heavy coat is draped over the back of a nearby sofa.

There is a quiet presence about Sabiryan, as one often senses with the deaf or blind. This, combined with his bald pate and gently lined face give him more the appearance of a Buddhist monk than the war hero and farm cashier that he was.

A few feet away is a table groaning with food. Before there can be any interview, the guests must first sit and consume a bowl of homemade *pelmeni*. "That's how we do it here, 15 per person," says Rishat, Sabiryan's son-in-law.

It turns out that Sabiryan can read Russian just fine with his one good eye, and even speak it, though in a very thick Tatar accent, clouded by a hoarse voice and slightly slurred tongue. Rashid shows him questions on an iPad and Sabiryan offers long stories in reply. His Russian is fleetingly intelligible, but mostly unclear. Thankfully, the family has an archive of his stories captured and written down some years earlier.

Sabiryan was born in this village in the fall of 1917, into a large family of twelve children, including two sets of twin boys.

What can I say?... The people were very poor... there was a revolution. Before the war, there were thatched roofs... Small houses... But the village was owned by rich people... In general, people started to live better.

Sabiryan began working in the local kolkhoz when he was just 15.

I was a bookkeeper in the kolkhoz administration. Marked down workdays. It's called an economist. Kept track of workdays of kolkhozniks before the war.

Just before he turned 21, Sabiryan was drafted into the army, to serve in the Far East. There, Russia and Japan were engaged in an undeclared war throughout the region, which Japan wanted to absorb into its Manchukuo Province.

At the end of August '38, they sent us from the village of Sakhayevo to the military draft office. That very same day we arrived in Ufa. There were guys from various regions of Bashkiria. They put us on a train to Vladivostok. We rode for a month. We arrived in Vladivostok and then they sent us on a ship over the sea to Khasan. We arrived at the military outpost of Khansi, on the banks of the Ussuri River. They attached us to the 107th artillery division. We were scouts for the border troops. They gave me a horse named Nagan ["Revolver"]...*

In 1940 several Red Army guys, now soldiers, were sent to Khabarovsk... to the 19th Light Tank Division. In the fall of that year I became a tank driver with the rank of junior sergeant...

After Germany attacked in June 1941, Sabiryan was sent west with his tank and brigade.

On November 1, 1941, we arrived at the Tikhvin junction station between Moscow and Leningrad. The cannonades of war were audible, we could hear the war. They disbursed us in the forest. They said to us: do not give up Tikhvin to the enemy. We covered the tanks with pine branches so that the Germans would not bomb us with their planes. But a fragment got me in the leg and I ended up in a hospital called Beliye Vorota. I lay there until December 1941. Then they broke up our unit and sent me to Smolensk Oblast, in an infantry unit.

In the cold January days of 1942, the Germans were on the defensive, and our guys started to attack, in order to straighten out the front line. We slept in the forest, buried in snow in our white coats. We would lie there during the day and attack at night.

---

* The Khansi border outpost is now known as Utinaya. Khasan is actually on the Tumannaya River, not the Ussuri, just across from present-day North Korea; at this time it was territory that had been occupied by Japan since 1910.

Sunflower fields stretch to the horizon beneath azure skies.

Sabiryan, left, during his military duty.

Right, Sabiryan with his wife and their first son, Khalit, born in 1949.
Below, Sabiryan and his immediate family members today.

After difficult battles, after the shooting stopped, we would come out of the snow and I would see bodies all around. I once came out of the snow and went into the forest. Not a single commander. Suddenly, nearby a shell exploded and I was thrown a long way from where I had been standing. Shrapnel had landed in my face. The medic came over and bound my head up in gauze. They dragged me to the medical station on a skid made from two skis. The next day I could not open my mouth, it was injured.

I wanted to eat, I was hungry, but could not talk. I could just signal with my hands what I needed. The medic served me up some thick soup.

After he recuperated, Sabiryan was sent with some 60 other tank drivers to Gorky (present-day Nizhny Novgorod) to learn how to drive American and British tanks that were sent over under the Lend-Lease aid program. Then, from 1944 through the end of the war, he fought in tank battles from the Carpathians into Eastern Europe.

I was given the rank of sergeant-major. And in August 1944 we went to the front in these tanks. I found out where I was only later, when I received my Red Army book [a record of service]. We attacked... through Poland and into Hungary. We battled in Hungary and liberated the city of Budapest. We forded the Danube on a pontoon bridge built of logs and headed in the direction of Austria.

March 15-20 was very hot, and in the fields the tanks began to bog down in the earth. So we drove only at night, along the banks of small rivers. As a result, by March 20 we had liberated the Germans' major defense points... On March 21, the Germans bombed us. A bomb fragment landed in my eye...

In the first medical unit, they looked at my eye and asked if they should remove it. I did not allow them... Then they sent me to another hospital, and there the surgeon explained that the fragment had not only landed in my eye, but in my skull, and that I could end up losing my second eye as well. So they fixed me up there and sent me back to my unit.

On the train, people were walking up and down, yelling that the war was over, that Germany had lost... They took us to Romania. That was around May 15. Any extra soldiers and commandants were sent to the Far East, to liberate China from the Japanese. And us, the wounded, were reassigned to the USSR Interior Troops, to bring order to the occupied territories... I served in a small city in Romania as a unit commandant... I was let out only in March 1946.

Three days after I returned to the homeland, I was invited to the kolkhoz administration and they made me a time-clock secretary and trusted me to work with funds.

The military report, by the way, according to which Sabiryan received his medal for gallantry, recounts the events of March 1945 less casually:

Sabiryan's family lays out a spread for visitors, including 15 pelmeni per person.

Sabiryan at rest.

> *Tank driver-mechanic... Sergeant-Major Sabir Zinnatovich Asfandiyarov... during his unit's military actions from March 4-21, 1945, took part in 12 successful attacks, during one of which he destroyed with his tank tracks an enemy cargo vehicle, three carts, and up to 10 Fritzes.*

Today, well into his retirement, Sabiryan is looked after by his energetic daughter Guzel and son-in-law Rishat. During the long, hot days out here on the steppe, he likes to sit in his garden and greenhouse, breathing in the warm, clean air, surely thinking about where his life has taken him.

Now my life is good. But before, all sorts of things happened. That's it.

A neighbor comes by and recounts how 360 men left the village for the war and only 120 came back, and that now Sabiryan is the last one alive.

"He is our last hero," the friend says.

That may be, but Sabiryan can't seem to understand what all the fuss is about. He left his Sakhayevo at 20, traveled from one end of the Eurasian continent to the other as a warrior, fighting Nazis from atop tanks, was thrice wounded, including losing an eye, and then returned to his home village to work for 30 years as a kolkhoz cashier.

And now, after 100 years of life, deaf, partially blind, and surrounded by a loving family and a beautiful countryside, he says everyone is asking him all these things that happened years ago, but he has an important question that he asks all the journalists who visit.

None of them, he says, are able to tell him what is going on in Loch Ness, and what it is that lives there.

A comparable conundrum was shared by Sabiryan's daughter, Guzel.

It seems that, during the Civil War of 1918-1922, Sabiryan's elder brother, Khabibulla Nigmatullin, fought with the Whites (not willingly, Guzel says) and retreated east with them through Siberia, finally ending up in Harbin, China.*

The brother disappeared without a trace.

But then, in the 1980s, a letter arrived in Sakhayevo from China with the question, "Do descendants of the Asfandiyarov family live here?" Sabiryan was summoned to the village administrative office and shown the letter. He disavowed it, said he did not know who it was from, and that he had no intention of answering it.

The thread was lost.

After the USSR fell apart, however, the family wrote a letter to the TV program, "Wait for Me," which tracks down stories like this, in hopes of relocating the familial thread stretched thin in the 1920s and then cut in the 1980s.

They never heard back.

---

* Harbin was a village in northeast China that, in the early 1900s, grew rapidly into a city to support and administer the Russian-financed Chinese Eastern Railway. It also served as Russia's base of operations during the 1904-1905 Russo-Japanese War. Over 100,000 White Russians and other émigrés fled to Harbin during the Bolshevik Revolution and Civil War, and it became the largest Russian enclave outside the Soviet Union.

MARIA FYODOROVNA RYLIK
MINSK
30 SEPTEMBER 1917

Minsk had been a part of the Russian empire for just 124 years when the 1917 revolution arrived. Gained from Poland in the Second Partition of 1793, it was a provincial backwater of fewer than 10,000 souls. But it grew quickly through the nineteenth century to five times that, with rapid industrialization making it a hotbed for political dissent: the first ever congress of the Russian Social Democratic Labor Party, which eventually split into the Bolsheviks and Mensheviks, took place in Minsk in 1898.

But, more than anything else, it is war that has shaped this city along the Svislach River, particularly the Second World War. Devastated by three years of German occupation, the Holocaust (Minsk was the site of a Nazi ghetto for 100,000 Jews), and relentless bombardment during that conflagration, Minsk went from a population of nearly 300,000 to less than 40,000, and was largely reduced to rubble. Then, after the war, the city was rebuilt in the imperial Stalinist style, with expansive prospects and avenues, kilometer-long apartment blocks, and official buildings boasting broad stairways and sweeping architectural lines. Today Minsk is home to two million.

On the top floor of a well-kept cement block apartment building not far from the city's impressive World War II Museum, Maria Rylik sits perched on the edge of a divan, her hair perfectly coifed, anxious to recount the stories of a century lived in Belarus. With gentle blue eyes and blonde-grey hair, Maria is like a human anti-incarnation of Minsk. Humble and self-effacing, regal in bearing and the opposite of ostentatious, she speaks matter-of-factly, without embellishments – it is a mien surely influenced by spending a third of her life

teaching, but one that also speaks to her unusual combination of village roots and urban, intelligentsia sophistication.

I was born in the village of Usmyn, Velikoluk Okrug – there was an okrug with that name then... Father was a priest and mother was at home, a housewife. But she too graduated from the gymnasium. She tried teaching, but it didn't work out for her. She was married, and she stopped working, she didn't like teacher's work. Yet I loved it, and did it for 36 years...*

We lived in the most common home... I remember we had a piano in the house... I had my own bedroom... But I was afraid to sleep there, especially when it stormed. I always tried to crawl into bed with Mama, or to get on her good side so I could lie down with her. I truly feared thunderstorms... Even now I fear them. But my sister was not afraid. It would storm and she would open the windows and sit near them. That's how brave she was...

There were me and my older sister, the oldest, and two brothers. One was born in 1905, Grigory, and Sergei in 1904. But they have all died. I am the only one left of that generation, there are no others. I am the last Mohican. [laughs]

But I loved my childhood. True, my mama died young, when I was about 7 or 8, and I was alone with my father. Then my father also died, and I was left, well, how can I explain it? I was brought up by very good, kind people. They turned me into a person, they taught me everything... how to work, how to interact with other people. They helped me in my studies; they all encouraged me to study... I completed the Byelorussian Teacher's Institute, and after that I got lazy. I could have studied a bit more... but I thought that I had already learned everything, that I needed to work.

This abbreviated version of Maria's history, however, leaves out an important chapter and a significant transition. For in Usmyn she was hindered from pursuing further education beyond the primary level because her father had been a priest.

Previously, among other things, they demanded a statement for fourth grade, or one for 7th or 10th grade. "Give us your biography and write out who your father was, and your mother, your grandfather." It was a long thing. Had to be a few generations. For certain you had to put down your mother's mother and father, but I don't recall if they required more...

Problem was, not only was Maria's father a priest, but her mother's and father's fathers were as well. So Maria says she altered her story a bit.

I said that my father was a teacher. Well, I thought that a priest and a teacher are sort of similar. Similar roles: to educate children. To educate people...

---

* See footnote, page page 100.

Maria's mother and father, 1894.

It was not a problem for my brothers, they finished. But I was not allowed to study. I finished four grades and that was it, nowhere else would take me... so my father hired a teacher, and I studied fifth, sixth, and seventh grades with him. And after that I moved to Byelorussia. Here I started learning in the Byelorussian language. I mastered it in six months...

The move was actually spurred by something else. Maria calls herself an orphan, as if her father died soon after her mother, yet the truth is Maria did not welcome her father's second marriage, which followed quickly after her mother's death. She speaks of two sisters in Usmyn, Pelageya and Akulina, who "saved her" when her "parents died," essentially adopting her. Yet her father lived on until at least the early 1930s.

In 1930 Maria moved to live with her older sister Alexandra, in a little room inside the school in the village of Kozulichi, near Bobruisk (Mogilev region). And, at some point after the move, her sister (as she herself had done) changed Maria's legal last name from Borisovich to Borisevich, likely because it sounded more Byelorussian but, more importantly, to make foggier the link with their father's priesthood.

It was not Maria's first time in Byelorussia. She had been there when she was younger, traveling with her mother, Zinaida, to help take care of Alexandra's new baby.

I fell in love with Byelorussia first of all because it was far warmer here than at home. At home, there would already be frost in November... but here it was warm, the leaves were still falling in November, only starting. I liked Byelorussia, and when the opportunity presented itself, I drifted away from there [the village where I was born]...

My sister was a teacher of younger grades, and I came to live with her until she died. When she died, some friends took me in and I lived with them until I got married. They gave me away. I got married in 1936... then I started living independently with my husband. And I took correspondence courses in the institute, first in the technical high school, then in the institute.

At school, Maria had fallen in love with one of her teachers, Mikhail Rylik. She had just finished up the seventh level at the secondary school, and then an eighth course was added. Mikhail was sent to be its teacher.

We would go out together, talk. We loved to talk about various things, which is why I liked him. There was no vulgarity, we had good conversations with one another. About our parents, our friends...

We met, became friends, fell in love with one another and got married. In 1936. My brother, the military colonel, came for the wedding. So everything was as it should be...

Our wedding was, well... My cavalier arrived... we took a bottle of vodka, some wine, appetizers... we sat around the table and ate and drank, and that's it. That was our wedding feast. Back then, they did not do wedding feasts. I said, "I don't need a feast." We lived well and had friends. Soon children started arriving... First a son before the war, and after the war, a daughter.

As for most people in this part of the world, for Maria, the war is a major dividing line in her life. Her husband had already been drafted to fight in the somewhat distant Finnish War (1939-40), but the German attack brought war directly into the family's home and land.

Oy, how the war began, it was awful. My father-in-law ran to fetch me. I lived in a village that was 55 kilometers from Mogilev, and 55 kilometers from Bobruisk. They lived in Bobruisk Rayon... The war had already begun. He ran 55 kilometers on foot, to see if I was still alive. And we left. I went to the chairman of the kolkhoz and asked for a horse, and they gave me a horse with a cart. And off we went. What did I take? Well, some sort of a chest, and a bit more. And my son. And we left there and lived in my husband's village. We survived, of course, that awful thing – war. I would not wish it on anyone.

The day after they took me away, our entire village was burned down... Oh, the horror.

She lived with her in-laws through the entire war, until 1946. It was distant enough from the main thoroughfares, Maria says, that they saw little of the Germans.

They all went on the [main] avenue and practically did not look our way. I was saved there. If I had not left, of course... The day after they took me away, our entire village was burned down... They burned the village down where my husband and I worked. And with it our bosses and everyone – oh, the horror. I could never go back there. They burned up all the people I knew, all of our friends, whose children I had taught... it was horrible...

But there were times, nonetheless, when the Germans did come to her in-laws' village. Including once when Maria was suffering from typhus.

We hid everywhere, wherever we could. We learned that Germans were somewhere in the district, and might come to where we were. We hid in the banya, in the field, everywhere. Some ran to the river, where there were some bushes. Anywhere you could hide, but thankfully we were not caught...

The Germans were doing round-ups, gathering up people, sending them to Germany and there doing with them whatever they liked. Some lived, some were burned up, others were raped, which is why we were afraid of ending up in Germany...

Some girlfriends and I ran off far into the fields, far from the road, far from one another. The main thing is one had to be vigilant. The war taught us to always be vigilant, in peacetime, but especially in wartime...

The news that the war was over arrived in rather dramatic fashion.

The first secretary of the Bobruisk Regional Committee, the party committee, arrived on a white horse. He arrived on a horse and told us that the war was over. So, of

A 1934-35 class picture. Maria is in the right bottom corner, Mikhail Rylik, her future husband, is in the center.

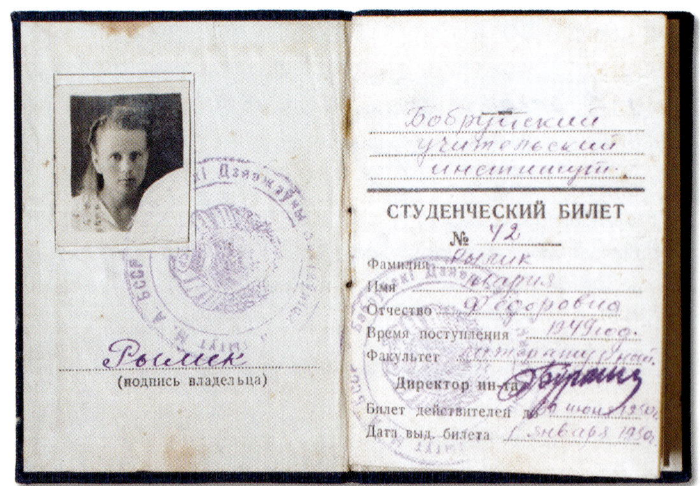

Бобруйский учительский институт

СТУДЕНЧЕСКИЙ БИЛЕТ

№ 42

Фамилия Рылик

Имя Мария

Отчество Федоровна

Время поступления 1949 г.

Факультет литературный

Директор ин-та

Билет действителен до [illegible] 1950 г.

Дата выд. билета 1 января 1950 г.

Рылик

(подпись владельца)

Maria's student ID booklet from 1949.

Maria and Mikhail with son Alexander in Germany, 1946.

Maria and with her daughter Regina, 1966.

course, we sang war songs and went to the village to celebrate with the young guys and girls. We were all so happy.

After the war ended, in 1947, Maria nonetheless found herself shipped off to Germany, only not as a prisoner, but as the wife of an occupying soldier in what would later become East Germany.

I lived in Germany for a year. Then my husband, you understand, did not want to serve any longer. He wanted to demobilize as soon as possible. So he resigned and we returned home, to Byelorussia.

But while there Maria was shocked and confused that the quality of life in defeated Germany was nonetheless better than in the victorious Soviet Union, and that the Germans she met were so different from those who had occupied Byelorussia.

I simply could not understand it. How they were as occupiers and how they were in Germany after the war. They were more humble than water, quieter than grass...

There were no problems there. You could go where you like. I found a job there, they opened Russian schools for officers' children. They invited me to work there. I didn't want to. I thought I needed some time to just rest from everything. From all the slaughter. But they convinced me, and I started work at the school...

And I did not want to leave, I wanted to live there a bit longer, in that good situation...

[When we went home] they gave us an entire train wagon and we brought some furniture and other things... Dresses... furniture, a cupboard... good chairs... and clothes – everything that we earned from our work... They paid us our salaries in German marks... They paid me 200 marks, which was a good salary back then...

Three decades of teaching in Bobruisk followed (Maria as a teacher and Mikhail as a school administrator), and then retirement in the late 1960s.

Can I really say anything bad about my husband?... He was good. A concerned, good father, a good husband, and a good son. He worried about his parents. In general, I never regretted marrying him. I had once told myself that I would marry a man five years older than me. And that's just what I got.

In 1992, her husband Mikhail (whose actual birth name was Mefodiy) died. Since then, Maria has led an active life, to say the least, taking a vigorous interest in the lives of her relatives, whether caring for them in their last days or helping them to make life changes.

"I don't remember my grandmother ever thinking about herself," says granddaughter Yuliya. "My grandmother is a catalyst in my life." In 2004, when Yuliya and her husband decided to make a change in their life and move from Minsk to Moscow, Maria joined them. "We bought three *platzcart* [third class] rail tickets to Moscow, and she came with us. We could not have done it without her, and she was almost 90! I can't remember her ever being self-concerned, but only concerned for others.

"Being a teacher all her life, she educated all her children and grandchildren. We all like reading thanks to her – she got me my first library card when I was three and pretty much taught me to read at that age."

Yuliya shares another telling story about her grandmother. Apparently, when Maria was 90, for her birthday she invited her friends to a party but had to meet some of them to help them navigate the metro. But then there was an accident when one of the women, unfamiliar with metro travel, fell on the escalator, and several of them tumbled down and were hurt, including Maria.

The ambulance driver took one look at Maria's passport (which of course showed her age), Irina says, and said they needed to take her to the hospital, but Maria refused, saying she was fine and would take a taxi home. Which she did. And so, when all her family came home for the party, there she was sitting in the apartment, her head bandaged up like Van Gogh, and shrugging off the incident as nothing important.

Today, in a proof of how life comes full circle, Maria has returned to the faith that ninety years ago limited her educational opportunities under the Bolsheviks, a faith that she tried to forget for a long stretch of her life history. She has become very religious and regularly reads Christian literature, and until recently was a regular parishioner at the Saints Peter and Paul Cathedral in Minsk.

Thus, in the apartment's small bedroom, there are icons and a stack of religious literature on the desk. And, on a neighboring shelf, there is a picture probably captured 50 years ago of Maria's husband Mikhail, wearing a smart suit and medals earned in the war. Surrounding the photo are complete hardbound collections of the works of Victor Hugo and Jack London.

Maria's desk.

VERA VLADIMIROVNA YEFIMOVA

SAMARA

SEPTEMBER 30, 1917

Vera Yefimova lives alone in a fourth-floor apartment in a crumbling walkup on the outskirts of Samara. The floors of her apartment are a bit dirty, as she cannot do housekeeping on her own and does not want to pay someone to do it for her. The kitchen and living room appear never to have been remodeled (aside from the new windows the city installed in honor of her 100 years), and yet Vera moved in here 49 years ago.

A very friendly and easy-going social worker, Nadezhda Zamotina, looks in on Vera two or three times a week, bringing groceries, helping with errands, checking her blood pressure. But there are limits to what she can do – she has 11 such confined elderly clients to check in on multiple times each week.

Yet Vera is agile and spry, she darts around the apartment with ease and says she even gets down to the local grocery, a Magnit outlet, when she really needs to.

I head down from the fourth floor. I can't be sitting around all the time, so I stomp. Stomp, stomp, stomp on my own. And sometimes, you know, I'm sitting, sitting, and there's no bread in the house... Well, then... So I think, what am I sitting for, let's head down to Magnit. And bit by bit, la-la, plop-plop-plop, I slowly get there.

The last time it was sugar that dragged me out – no getting round it, there's not much sugar left, I thought. Need me a kilogram of sugar. A loaf of bread and some sugar... I go and go, and someone from our entrance says, "Vera Vladimirovna, let me carry that."

"Here you go, carry it. Take it up and hang it on my door. I'll climb up."

That's how it is. So, I walk. But I don't go to the hospital on my own. It comes around on its own, but rarely. I treat myself.

Vera has an expressive, gravel-tinged voice. She speaks clearly, but in phrases thick with colloquialisms and slang. "She is a complex person," says Nadezhda, "everything must be done according to her rules."

She greets her guests with a cheerful hospitality and a dry sense of humor. And she is not short on words. A single question invariably leads to a long and complex story, often capped with a sentence like, "Well, that's that." Or, "Now you know all there is to know."

My parents were of peasant stock, and rural and urban cabbies. * *That's my parents' parents. My parents were already literate office workers. Educated as a scribe my father was, and Mother also studied... There's no villagers amongst us, we're all city dwellers... As you see, I am myself a Samaran. I was born here, and I will die here.*

Her father fought in the Civil War, and the family was relocated with him when he was sent to work on the Tashkent Rail Line. Vera was four and five years old at the time.

And what do you think I remember? A lake that was at the station where we were, fish in the lake, and how we lived in an earthen hut. I remember going home to the earth. That's what. That's what I remember from the years '23, '22 and '21... Father was constantly working, he did not have an official job. There was horrible joblessness back then, horrible. There was only work starting in '27... He hauled stuff for a store, not officially, he just worked as a loader. Took this there, took stuff to the station. And in '27 he was offered literate work, and we started to settle in, we started to live... and Mama also had literate work, she worked in the Maslennikov factory...

Me, I studied, I started when I was 10, not seven, but 10. Because Mama was without a job, and Father too... Oh, I remember our first New Year's tree, that was in '26... and I remember the 30s... In '27 there was the first radio, and I heard that... and in fifth grade, I was already doing social work. In fifth grade they made us teach illiterate people. I went to this woman and taught her to read letters and to write numbers.

That's all. I'm already grown up now.

But an early memory, one of her earliest, plagues Vera. The 1930s were a difficult time, and children were made to do things that many are no longer proud of.

It's not pleasant to say. But necessary. But maybe don't write it down. It's not in fashion now. But back then it was very much in fashion... We lived in a rural area. Father worked, and they ruined a church. And they took the icons from the church...

---

* *Izvozchik*, literally, one who hauls or carries. Usually, this was someone with a horse hooked up to a carriage or cart.

Пролетарии всех стран, соединяйтесь!

ПОД ЗНАМЕНЕМ МАРКСИЗМА-ЛЕНИНИЗМА, ПОД РУКОВОДСТВОМ КОММУНИСТИЧЕСКОЙ ПАРТИИ–ВПЕРЕД, К ПОБЕДЕ КОММУНИЗМА!

ПОЧЕТНАЯ ГРАМОТА

НАГРАЖДАЕТСЯ

ЕФИМОВА ВЕРА ВЛАДИМИРОВНА

За долголетнюю добросовестную работу и активное участие в общественной жизни комбината – в честь международного праздника – ПЕРВОЕ МАЯ.

Директор комбината

Секретарь партбюро

Председатель завкома

28 апреля 1967г.

ПРОФИЗДАТ

Vera's honorary certificate for conscientious work and participation in public life. Below right, Vera in her youth.

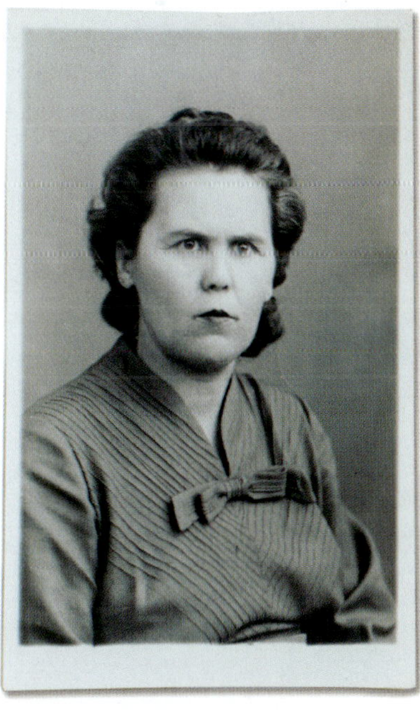

A clear memory sticks with me that we took those icons from the church. It was fourth and fifth graders...

After seven years of schooling, Vera started to work at the factory, when she was 19, having worked at other jobs since she was 17, including in a telegraph office, where she received and transcribed telegrams.

Then Father came to me and said, "Verushka, you're sitting all alone here, no young fellows, no one will see you sitting alone. Leave this."

"But where to?" I said.

"As a typist in the cadre department at the factory, where I work, where Mama works."

And they took me on there, since I was already working as a typist.

After three years at the factory, she met the man who would be her husband "on the way into and out of the factory," and they were married. That same year a son was born.

Yes, there was a wedding. Friends were there, his relatives were there. But it was so modest because it was a difficult year. 1939, before the war and all that. Difficult. For two years my mother-in-law watched my son, and after two years I started taking him to daycare.

Back then they sent out a decree: one month, two months. Sit at home, then return to work. And I took two months and returned to work. My mother-in-law stayed home. I ran home at lunch, fed him, then back to the factory. Within an hour, two hours.

Then I changed my shift and was able to be home two hours earlier... It was difficult to support a little boy. There were ration cards, bread. Water to be carried. There was no water, no firewood. Had to heat the stove. You come home and have to go out for wood, because you have to stoke the stove, and you have to take your ration card and buy some food.

And then the war came.

On that day I was... in the banya... On that day, in June, we were expecting my brother from Poltava, on his vacation. He'd finished military school, the Poltava Military High School. He'd sent a letter: "I'm getting a break. I'm coming home." And we went, Mama and me with the child, from the izba (we lived in a private home). We go through the gate and my 18-year-old brother runs up, yelling:

"Come greet the war!"

Mama says, "What, has he arrived?"

"Oh, no… War has broken out!"

Mama sat down and cried and we never received any news of my brother's fate.

Vera rests after her video interview.

The Volga River in Samara.

*My younger brother worked in the factory too, as a lathe operator. He worked until they took him into the army as well, at 18. In September they took him into the army. And then Mama and I were alone.**

...I remember 1941. It went like this: morning in the nursery, the day at work, after work looking for bread, for water, again firewood, firewood, again water, again into the garden. The whole war was like that. We lived somehow. Everything that was available, anything we had acquired, we sold, sold in the first two years. Everything. Then we started up with commerce. In the third year, we started to learn commerce. What can you do? The villagers arrive bringing sunflower seeds, you buy seeds, roast them on the stove, and at night you sit, selling seeds. And in the morning you go to work. That's what we did...

The reason I have lived to be 100 is because I was constantly working.

Even her relaxation was found in work.

A dacha for 35 years. A dacha. 35 years I had a dacha. That was my relaxation... I could not go to dances, I had a son to raise. I could not drink a glassful, I had a son to raise... We went to the theater when there were group trips... but there was no kind of entertainment... no, no, no... I sat at home, sewed, knitted, read what my son had written...

The happiest day in her life, Vera says, was when the war ended.

The happiest day was when the rationing system ended. And everything else was fine, as it should be.

Vera's marriage, however, did not last the war.

He had to serve. He served. Then: "I'm coming home soon." And he arrived home and said... He left me for a woman from the front.

Work became her refuge. Other than her son, it was her main reason for living. After she retired in 1972 from the factory's cadre department, after 20 years working there, they gave her a pension of just 80 rubles. She couldn't live on that, so she went to see the bosses and asked them to give her some kind of part-time work, as a custodian or a guard. But they refused. That was just not done, they said. So she found work as a common laborer in the bookbinding department. There she worked for another five years, in order to increase her pension.

All of my work, there was nothing special about it. But the good thing I did in my life was that I raised a son...

---

* The fate of Vera's father was unclear, but she said that during the war at one point he went to do a job in some distant location and never returned.

Her son, Yuri, finished seven years of schooling, but not easily, and then decided he'd rather go into the trades, so he became a worker on the railways. After two years work, he was called up to the military.

He went into the army. Served three years. At 20 he went in as a healthy boy, he rode a bicycle. And he left the army with a stomach ulcer. From the army, he entered an evening institute. Finished the evening institute, worked and studied, and got treatment. He died after his third operation: stomach cancer. 52 years old. 40 years labor seniority.

That was the unhappiest year in her life, she says. Even worse than the war. And, as if that were not enough, she was also caring for her sick mother at the time.

It was bad. Mama was paralyzed. She lay here. My bed was there, and she lay here. But she was sick. And my life ended. I was 70 when my son had his first operation, and Mama lay sick from a heart attack... And my son was yet to die, and then Mama died. * *And I was left alone, alone.*

Sadly, the death of her son led to a loss of all ties with her son's family.

When the father died, the grandchildren were no more. Who wants to live with two old women. Two old women. I was in my early 70s, and Mama was 90. Who needs them? I coped on my own. And I do that even now.

Perhaps then it is not surprising that Vera does not attribute her long life to a supportive family or to her community, but to work. To her "love of work."

I won't say anything else. But artists, they slather on make-up, and I didn't do that, and I don't have any wrinkles. [laughs] Bags, wrinkles. But I don't have any, everything has dried up, everything.

It is one of her self-deprecating jokes, covering sadness with humor.

What should I do, cry? Sometimes I cry, sometimes I joke. No one hears. You cry, and no one hears you, no one can make you feel better.

When I was 80, 25 people came to my birthday... They sat one atop the other here. But this year, no one remains. There is no one...

And with that, she decides the interview is over, that it is time to move on. It is time for tea.

And now we will feast. What, are we not people? I may be 100, but I am still a person. [laughs] I am a person. What about it? I will spread a white tablecloth for you.

And now we will feast. What, are we not people?

* She lived to be 99.

MARINA IVANOVNA GONCHAROVA
TARUSA, KALUGA OBLAST
25 NOVEMBER 1917

Tarusa is a small, provincial town just barely inside the border of Kaluga Oblast, nestled on a gentle bend in the Oka River. Quiet dirt roads amble down to the riverside through unkempt forests and neighborhoods full of colorful, wooden houses. There is a bus stop sinking into the earth, a small chapel and spring where locals draw their water, and a picturesque church that rises from a hill at the town's southern edge. A modern cafe perches above the river, offering cold drinks, good food, and a relaxing view of the central Russian landscape.

It is the sort of place one might expect a short story by Bunin or Chekhov to play out. In fact, Tarusa is a rather literary town, the subject of numerous poems, stories, and memoirs. The writers Konstantin Paustovsky and Nikolai Zabolotsky lived here, as did other luminaries, from Vasily Polenov to Svyatoslav Richter. And in the 1970s the town was the residence for many important dissident writers, for it lay just beyond Moscow's sanctified 100-kilometer radius, within which those exiled from the capital could not live.

At the ulitsa Lenina end of the town's diminutive river walk (near where there once stood a statue of Stalin, but where Lenin now holds court) there are statues of the poets Marina Tsvetaeva (whose family had a home here*) and Bella Akhmadulina, the latter sculpted by artist Boris Messerer, who was married to Akhmadulina.

---

* The poet also reputedly wanted to be buried here, at the confluence of the Tarusa and Oka rivers.

Marina Goncharova.

Marina's granddaughter, also Marina.

"I adore these places," Messerer wrote of Tarusa. "The central Russian landscape. In my opinion, there is no better place in Russia. One is attracted by its beauty, its nature, its expanse."

Marina Goncharova, despite her last name,* did not come to Tarusa for the town's literary connections. She simply moved to Tarusa (population 9,302) to be closer to her daughter after her husband died.

Confined to a wheelchair that she occupies with considerable dignity, Marina gets out little these days, yet enjoys long afternoons sitting in the sunshine of her walled-in porch. She takes great care to look good for her guests, fussing over her hair and makeup with her granddaughter, who shares her first name.† The two are strikingly similar, with attractive, round faces, and an elegant, self-assured demeanor. But whereas granddaughter Marina's speech has a soft, feminine timbre, babushka Marina's voice carries the wear of a century's aging and the monotone diction of one who has all but lost her hearing.

There is no better place in Russia. One is attracted by its beauty, its nature, its expanse

My mother had seven of us. I was the second. In our childhood we, well, we were not a rich family, but we were also not poor. Father, when I was born, was a sailor. He served in Leningrad and Kronstadt. He did his four years military service and then three years extra. Yes. We went with Mama to be with him... I was four years old and really liked it there.

But what else is there to say? I don't know. I studied in school, but not very well, because Mother had little time for me. She had little time for anything. She had small children and the household to care for. I arrived home from school, tossed my bag aside, and went outside to play. I was an Octobrist, it was that time. Then a Pioneer, then a Komsomolka, then a member of the Party.‡

In point of fact, in the year of Marina's birth, her father, Ivan Baranov, played a rather active part in Russia's revolutions. For he served in the Baltic Fleet aboard the *Emperor Pavel I*, whose sailors instigated a bloody mutiny in Helsinki on March 3, 1917, after receiving word of the tsar's abdication.

You know, perhaps he spoke of it, but I was a child. It wasn't interesting to me. He told stories about something or other to the grown-ups, but I just remember that he said he took part in the storming of the Winter Palace. That I do remember. And he served in Kronstadt. There were often various sorts of outbursts there... I was a child...

Soon after the revolution, Marina's family moved back to Simbirsk Gubernia, where her father and mother had been born.

---

* Ivan Goncharov authored the famous novel *Oblomov*, about a do-nothing superfluous man.

† Actually, the elder Marina was born Matryona, but she changed her name.

‡ All age-centered Party groups. The Octobrists were for children 7-9 years old; Pioneers was for children 10-15; the Komsomol was for youths 14-28.

Marina's parents, Ivan Stepanovich Baranov, and his wife, Alexandra Pavlovna.

The young family in Kamchatka, Maria and Alexander, and their daughter Yelena, born in 1944.

Marina in her military uniform.

He did not want to live in Leningrad any longer. He wanted to go home. And to work in agriculture. But he was literate and then he had been in the navy for seven years, he was advanced, not stupid... At first, Father worked, then he was elected chairman of the village council. Then he was director of a sawmill factory in a different village... and for the rest of his years he worked as the head of a kolkhoz. They would send him to kolkhozes that were having trouble. He got them back in shape, helped them. But what is interesting is that when he retired he had been paid all his working life not a salary, but in kind – in wheat and other goods. So he got a pension of just 19 rubles... He objected and tried to get it recalculated, but they would not...*

So her father got work in a local brick factory, not as a director, but as a humble watchman, at a miserly wage.

We did not live badly. In our village in 1930 and 1931, there were hungry years. It was difficult, of course, but then things started to get sorted out... The most important thing was that we had a cow. There was milk, tvorog, sour cream, and that was a huge support for the family. Chickens, our eggs, we had a garden, apples, pears, cherries, potatoes. That's how we lived.

I still remember how the first tractor arrived in our village. People ran after it, looking at it like it was a marvel. The [movie] theater was mobile, it arrived from the regional center to show us the pictures...

Granddaughter Marina interjects, "Grandma saw the first light bulb show up in the village, the first tractor. So, you could say she lived in the era of rushlights.† Under rather primitive conditions... Now my son is studying in Munich and we talk with him together over Skype – grandma with her earphones on the internet. That is something."

When I finished fourth grade in the village, I asked Mother and Father to set me up in the center of the administrative district, to get me an apartment. Well, they didn't object to me studying. So they set me up in an apartment with girls I studied with. But every Saturday I had to return home, to wash in the banya. It was 15 kilometers. And sometimes I had to walk alone. Three kilometers through the forest. There were wolves in the forest, and it was very scary... I will remember that all my life... But I overcame it, you know. For three years I walked those 15 kilometers every Saturday. And on Sunday I returned with a bag on my back full of produce. Mother would cook me something. After all, you have to eat.

Upon finishing ninth grade, Marina matriculated at the Chistopol Worker's Medical Faculty, where she studied for two years. And then, in 1935, she began

---

* Pensions in Russia were and are based on what one was paid during one's working life.

† A rushlight is a very inexpensive sort of candle or miniature torch.

Marina adjusts her makeup in advance of her photo shoot.

Tarusa.

her studies at the medical institute in Kazan. It was there she met her first love, Alexander Plastov.

I was in my second year, he was in his third. He was shy about meeting me, so he asked another girl to introduce us. And so we met. It was pure young love. Then he proposed to me. He said, "I can work as a feldsher. I will... I will find work. And we will live." But I was terribly afraid of getting married. I was 19 then, 18 or 19. I said no, that I would not get married until I finished the institute. And so we dated for three years. Then he finished the institute and went to Perm to work. From there they drafted him into the army. He served two years in the army and we wrote back and forth. We wanted to get married. But he did not succeed in getting discharged before the war began.*

When the Germans attacked, Alexander was serving in a rifle division, and they were immediately sent to the front lines and then just as immediately surrounded before they had a chance to fight. So their commander told them to try to escape any way they could.

He got out. I didn't know anything, we didn't write. It wasn't possible then, letters would take six months to arrive. I didn't know anything about him for so many years. I didn't know anything.

"Her entire life," granddaughter Marina interjects.

Then I found out that he escaped the encirclement and worked as the senior doctor [at a birthing hospital] somewhere near Vitebsk. As a gynecologist. Which he never really did. He treated the wounded. Vitebsk was occupied. It was very... they had to hide them, to put up signs. They hid communists and wounded [soldiers] and then treated them at night.

"He hid partisans and Red Army soldiers," granddaughter Marina adds. "The Germans regularly visited the hospital. He risked his life hiding these fighters, under beds or other places."

They would put up signs: "Typhus". They were afraid. "Births in progress" – that's the sort of signs they would put up.

But soon their ruse was found out, the Germans overran the hospital and executed the "patients," and Alexander fled to fight with the partisans. In 1942, when he was on a mission to bomb a train, he was ambushed and killed.

They captured him and shot him. And his mother didn't know. She didn't know about her son for 37 years... He was honored after his death. His portrait hangs in some city there; he is a hero of Belorussia...

In the army, he got married. And he had a daughter. Her father never met her. The daughter grew up and studied to be an engineer. There were grandchildren... and one

---

* A village primary care physician.

of the grandchildren told the grandmother all of this. They didn't know anything. After many years they found out that he had died with the partisans.

Marina, meanwhile, was in the Mordovian Republic, very close to Nizhny Novgorod (then known as Gorky), when the war broke out.

It was Sunday, a very nice day. I had a friend who was a doctor and she and her husband came to see me in the morning, saying, "Let's go to the bazaar." We went to the bazaar, bought some produce, and we were walking past a club near our place, and there were lots of lilacs around the club. So we picked some lilacs and walked home with them. We went into my place – I rented a small room and there were [radio] speakers in the rooms, these round black things. Suddenly we hear Molotov speaking. And he declares that Germany, that Germany attacked us. I was so afraid that I cried. Then, a few days later, the military commander said to me, "Be prepared: they can call you up in 10 minutes." And that's how it was.

The military commander said to me, "Be prepared: they can call you up in 10 minutes." And that's how it was.

When the call came, Marina was collected with other doctors in Saransk – a brigade of about 20, then put on a train heading east. It went slowly, stopping frequently to let through trains full of soldiers coming from the East to fight the Germans.

I remember, we went to the river, the train stopped by a river, and we washed up there, our face and feet. And we stopped near the Angara. We went swimming, but the water was like ice. It was impossible, it was all we could do just to wash up... They took us to Khabarovsk and we swam in the Amur. The Amur was clean then, warm, very nice. We lived there two weeks, waiting for a ship. Then they took us to Vladivostok... There they assigned us to various places: some to Kamchatka, some to Sakhalin... and I ended up in Kamchatka.

When we left Vladivostok early in the morning, it was still dark. It was not a passenger ship, but it was sort of converted for passengers. There were beds and double bunks. I felt like I would be ill. So I jumped up and saw that other doctors had also jumped up. And we all began to be sick, it was so bad. That's when I found out what it meant to rock on the sea. The Okhotsk Sea is very rough.

Then, when we were sailing near Japan, two or three airplanes appeared above us. We thought they would bomb us, but they just circled, looked at something or other, and flew off. Then they returned again. It was very scary. They didn't let any of us up on deck. But the planes didn't drop anything on us. We arrived safely on Kamchatka and I was struck by its beauty. The Lyubov Hill[*] *– right on the ocean. A very beautiful place. Ships were anchored, the bay was so beautiful.*

---

* Literally "the Hill of Love"; it is located in Petropavlovsk-Kamchatsky and its official name is Nikolskaya Hill.

Marina was a young, inexperienced doctor and the workload was tremendous. She recalls how they were immediately issued uniforms sized for men that made them "look like puppets." They learned to handle and shoot weapons, dug an underground ward to be safe from bombings, and of course treated wounded soldiers and prisoners.

It was, the most difficult time in my life. It was anything but easy.

There were few medicines, treatment was very difficult, and no foreign medicines at all. The hospital did not even have an X-ray machine. I was blind. Then an order came down. There was some high mortality rate or such, and we were to do autopsies on all soldiers that died. And there in my ward lay this soldier with abscesses on his lungs. He was sick for three months and then he died. And I had to do the autopsy.

I still remember with horror how I was completely inexperienced, and yet unable to refuse. And I could be injured myself. I had no experience. I had never done an autopsy. But I agreed to do it. It was very scary... they had only shown us once, when I was a student.

There were many difficulties, but after the war things eased up... 1943, 1942, those were very meager years. Everything was dried: dried potatoes, dried egg powder. They gave us rations. Dried milk... Everything was dried. We did not see potatoes, tomatoes. Fish and cheremsha [wild garlic] are what saved us. But my husband and I didn't really like fish and preferred not to eat it.

It was in Kamchatka that Marina met her husband, Alexander Goncharov.

Well, we had classes in the medical battalion. He, I noticed, was constantly looking at me, constantly trying to start a conversation. We got acquainted. But we didn't date, nothing like that.

Then, later, when they transferred me to the fifth construction site, there was a coincidence, he was a divisional doctor and he was also transferred to the construction site as a doctor. And there we met again. Well, we started to date... there was a little bit of time after work. And, well, then we were married. About four or five months after we met. He was a captain.

...He was a very jealous husband... I was always very modest, I never had any lovers, even though many chased me. But he was horribly jealous. Even the commissar of the regiment, when we were driving to the aerodrome one time, said to me, "I watch you, you are so modest. Women in the army are generally very loose, but we have no criticisms of you. You live a normal life."

But life was anything but normal for a Soviet military physician. You went where they sent you, did as you were ordered, and had few possessions. But the reward of saving lives served to even up the scales. Marina recalls how, while in Kamchatka, she happened upon a boy who had drowned in the river, and some boys were pulling him out. She ran to him and did mouth-to-mouth.

And we brought him back to life. He was completely dead, had turned blue, was not breathing. Water flowed out of his mouth and he came back to life. I guess that I saved him.

Or there was the time with the injured Japanese prisoner of war with a seriously swollen hand.

He fell to his knees in front of me and started to explain that he had this, and this, and this child. He asked me to save him, that he had to raise his children. Well, we saved him, did an incision, cleared out the puss, and his hand came back to life.

She smiles when remembering the day that peace finally came:

We heard about it, we screamed, we were happy, we jumped around.

The couple (and their daughter, Yelena, born in 1944) left Kamchatka in 1948, re-assigned to Engels, near Saratov.

When we arrived in Vladivostok... they put us up in a hotel. And in the morning my daughter and I woke up – there were no beds, we were assigned a couch – and what did we see before our eyes? We had not seen tomatoes for so many years. And here were big, beautiful tomatoes. My husband had gotten up early, gone out and bought them. I looked at them, and my daughter said, "Mama, what are those?" She had never seen tomatoes. She was four years old.

After a few years in Engels, they were re-assigned to a sanatorium in Kudeptsa, near Sochi. But despite the change to warmer climes, the work was not good. Alexander did not like the sanatorium, saying that "everyone from the boss down to the waiters is stealing goods, and the patients complain of the bad food."

It was in Kudeptsa that Marina went into labor with her second child. She remembers the episode in her characteristically matter-of-fact style.

It happened at night when my husband was far away... there was no hospital. He went to find a car, a driver. And while he was gone, my daughter was born. It's a good thing that the neighbor's daughter was with me. I birthed her, my daughter, cut the cord myself, tied it off myself. I cleaned her up myself, swaddled her. That's how it happened.

A transfer to Grozny soon followed, and there the couple was happier, working there until their retirement in the 1970s. Marina resisted the urge to leave until Alexander's death in 1987.

The Chechens had already arrived in Grozny. We lived there for many years, for 28 years we lived in Grozny. But it became very difficult. Back when they first arrived – they arrived by train – they were peaceful, respectful. But when the Chechen Repub-

*lic was formed, they started to do outrageous things, they started killing people whom they did not feel were important. It became very scary to live there.**

Moving to live with her daughter and son-in-law has proven a blessing, but being immobilized in a wheelchair has its challenges in a society that makes little accommodation for the disabled. Granddaughter Marina recounts how during the winter her babushka chipped a tooth, and the sharp edge began to scrape the inside of her mouth. They tried to get a local dentist to come around for a visit, but could not. So finally Marina the younger went to the hardware store, got a metal file, and then came back and filed down her grandmother's tooth.

Good stories or bad, the two Marinas love to spend time together reminiscing.

Yes, we often reminisce about all our people. My oldest daughter died four years ago. My youngest is still alive, but she is sick. I had two children, two daughters. Four grandchildren, one great-granddaughter, and five great-grandsons.

"They come here and you beat them at cards, no?" granddaughter Marina says smiling, speaking of her sons, her babushka's great-grandsons. The great-babushka laughs/

Yes, they come to visit. Both great-grandsons are very nice to me.

---

* In 1944, Stalin had all the Chechens and Ingush – nearly 500,000 souls – deported from Chechnya. After Stalin's death, and with liberalization, some were allowed to slowly return, but, in many cases, their homes and land had been occupied by settlers from the North. The end of the USSR in 1991 led to a Chechen independence movement that devolved into two bloody wars, one from 1994-1996, and a second from 1999-2000.

Paul Richardson, Mikhail Mordasov, and Nadya Grebennikova in Moscow, with Galina and Irina Grebneva.

INSTEAD OF A CONCLUSION

There may be no better way to sense one's mortality than to be in contact with the infinite or transcendent: to stand in an empty field at midnight and soak in the stars from horizon to horizon; to sit in a quiet rural church and commune with its makers and one's own; to float on a placid sea so far from shore that the watery horizon is unbroken in every direction.

Someone who has lived 100 years may not be infinite, but given how far their lifespan is beyond the norm for these people, in these times, in this place, it is nonetheless a transformative experience to meet with them. All of us taking part in this project have been changed: we have come away with a deepened respect and appreciation for the elderly, for the importance of family and community, for the fragility of memory. We can only hope that this book, these stories, will convey to readers a fraction of the power we felt.

Together, we three traveled over 20,000 kilometers across the former dominions of the Russian empire. We were welcomed into humble, cozy private spaces and trusted with moving family stories that left us with new perspectives on our history. It is one thing to read about World War II or Collectivization, another thing entirely to meet a partisan or a kulak, a war hero or a home front laborer, and to hear their stories first-hand, to hear how they built and lived their lives.

Interestingly, even in this relatively small sample of centenarians, we kept tripping over similar strings: Baskiria, kulaks, chicory, Rybinsk, palki and Kaluga. And we also were able to compile a catalog of shared traits and advice on what one must do to live a hundred years. Here it is:

- Work hard from an early age. Manual labor is particularly beneficial, especially very difficult physical labor. Do it all your life.
- Take pleasure and pride in your work.
- Be optimistic and pleasant. Don't waste time on pointless unpleasantries.
- Focus on doing good, on being sincere.
- Don't drink much and don't overeat.
- Stay out of hospitals. If you suffer a serious injury or debilitation, don't let it define you. Keep going.
- Cultivate grit. Know what you want and keep at it. The best way to overcome incredible hardships and difficulties is through sheer force of will and resilience.
- Have blue eyes.
- Maintain a comparatively low blood pressure.
- Be lucky.

This project also reminded us not to be deceived by appearances, and we quickly learned that the people we saw during our visits were but a narrow reflection of their fuller reality. A few examples that readers should recognize from the preceding texts:

An elderly man who can barely hear and speak, hobbling around his apartment. Once, he was an active naval seaman who fought and was captured as a prisoner of war, surviving years of misery. He then spent much of his life living off the grid.

A lithe, elderly woman, smartly dressed and a very graceful dancer. She spent most of her working life in textile mills.

A wheelchair-bound woman who lives alone and has no family. In her youth, she was a member of a traveling acrobatic group.

Two quiet, serene men who spend their days in their gardens. One was a sapper on the outskirts of the Leningrad Blockade, the other chased Nazis atop American-made tanks and was thrice wounded in the war.

A blind, seemingly helpless, but very cheerful woman who spends her days in a room surrounded by pictures and mementos she cannot see. In her youth, she was a diplomat's wife, a teacher, and a very skilled table tennis player.

No project of this scope and ambition ever goes where you expect. We began the Children of 1917 Project thinking that the result would be something like a rich tapestry: a history of the past century woven from the stories of two-dozen heroes' lives. Of course, there is some of that. But the final result is less the history of a country through the prism of private lives, and more about private stories of resilience in the face of one of the most difficult centuries in a country's life.

Thank you to all who have supported and encouraged this project in countless ways visible and invisible. Your gifts have been a priceless contribution.

Paul Richardson
Mikhail Mordasov
Nadya Grebennikova

PROJECT BACKERS

Crowdfunding flips conventional publishing on its head.

In the normal publishing paradigm, a company or individual dreams up an idea, marshals the authors, contributors, and ideas, and then packages them into a product and tosses it out onto the market, hoping for a positive response. With crowdfunding, you pitch an idea, and if there is sufficient positive response, all the other bits follow. If not, the idea dies for lack of funding.

That the idea for this project was able to become a reality is directly attributable to the 300+ backers listed on these pages. They are due a special thanks for their faith in the value of this project when it was just an idea, for their trust in us as creators, and for their patience while we executed on the plan. We hope to have satisfied their expectations.

ASSOCIATE PRODUCERS

Alexei and Yuliya Bolshakov

SPONSOR

Raiffeisen Bank Russia

CO-SPONSORS

Anonymous

Ricki Slattery Starrett

DIRECTORS

Harlan and Ellen Ratmeyer

SUPPORTERS

Anonymous (multiple)
Neale Ainsfield
Moonyeen Albrecht
Vicki Albu
Clyde Alexander
Irina Amosova
Janet Anderson
Kyle Anniko
Natasha Antonov
Maria Antonova
James W. Armstrong-Wood
George S. Artemoff
Lucy Ash
Allegra Azulay
Ernest Barnett
Mona Baroudi
Robert Barrett
Gary R. Basham
Sergei Belov
Michele A. Berdy
Kate Beswick
James Biedron
Mary Jane Bolin
Anders Bolinder
Evert Jan Bos
Victoria Bosh
Alice Anna Bota
Jack and Caroline Brickley
M Brierley
Elizabeth A. Brock
Deborah Brower
Malcolm Hamrick Brown
Jim and Sandy Buch
Ben and Patricia Buchholtz
Justin Bunnell
Alexander Burak
Elizabeth Butler
John Campo
Dr. Edward Carberry
Lucy Carr
Jennifer Ann Casey
Catherine Cauvin-Higgins
Natalya Chernobrovnika
K. JoAnn Clendenen
Bob and Ginger Clough
Marie Cochineas
Donna Collins
Jeff Concors
Ricardo Contreras Jr.
Alex Cook
Melenaite Cook
BreeAnn Cossitt
David and JoEllen Cowee
The Cupples-Kruse Family
Jon R Daugherty
Elizabeth Davis
E.B. Davis
DH Deprimo
Megan L. Dixon
Leigh Dolin
Lisa Donoghue
Lilian Dregalla
Chris Duffy
Kathy Duggan
Lorenzo Dutto
D. Dykeman
Tamara Eidelman
Svetlana Elfimova
Tom Elliott
James Elwood
John Enders
Greogry Engel
Christine Ertl
Maria Evans
Elena Everitt
Marina Evteeva
Nora Favorov
Kathryn Fern
Errol and Mary Louise Flynn
Sibelan Forrester
Elisabeth J Fox
Jewel Fox
George A. Freeman
K. Fresnel
RD Gale
Sarah Woodside Gallagher
Jill Gammon
Alexander Gayvoron
Suren Gazaryan
Anton Genkin
Erika Goff
Gabriele Goldstone
Olga Golubkova
Nadezhda Goncharova
Andrei Gordasevich
James Peter Gregora
Neil M Gridley
Jeremy Griffin
Rachel Grmela
Elizabeth Geacintov Guest
Sean Guillory, SRB Podcast
Mark & Lynn Gwynn
Scott K. Haight
Jeffrey Hanson
Krista Hanson

Elaine Hasty
John Wesley Hawes
Glenn Hellrud
Jeff Hensley
Alex Herlihy
RK Hoffmann
C. Christopher Hook, MD
Kathy Howard
Yvonne Howell
Will Hubin
Svein Hvile
Thomas Irmer
Yevgeny Ivanov
Ange J.
Lucia Ferris Jacobs
Jakki
Robin Je
Mandy Jenkinson
Mary C. Jess
Ali Johnson
Allyn Johnson
Ramzan Kadyrov
Judith Kalb
Mindie Jeanne Kaplan
Zurab Kazbegi
Maria Khodykina
Alisa Khomyanina
Kathleen Kinsey
Carol Kitamura
Ann Kleimola
Natalya Kolesnikova
Dorsey Kordick
Dmitry Kotov
Heidi L. Kreuzer
Ruth Hinkle Kreuzer
Kristina
Christel Krugovoy
Walter Kuball
Yelena Kulikova
Jim Kurtz
Tatyana Kurylenko
Victoria Kutukova
Michael A. Kuzmiak III
Annette La Rosa
Catherine Landers
Brian R. Larsen
Jean Lauderdale
Brittanie Leibold
Jesse and Alyssa Leggoe
Pattie Leonardis
Charles Letourneau
Olga Li
Brenda Lipson
LP
Ian Luyt
C Lythgoe
Jean M.
Tara Macias Serfaty
Elaine MacKinnon
Norman MacPhee
Daniel Main
Alexei Malgavko
Malia Mallchok
Marisha
Garrett J McClintock
Jim McHugh
Thomas E. and Judy Hill McHugh
Elizabeth McLaughlin
Carolyn and David Meisel
Alina Melnikova
Dwight & Alisa Mengel
Peter Merrill
MIR Corporation
Anastasia Mitsul
Andrew Molboski
Peter Morley
Jeanette E. Morris
Maka Morris
Scott D. Moss
Carl Mountford
Debbie Newman
Sandy Newman
Laura Cassano Nicholas
Mary Nicholas
Nina
Marita Nummikoski
Lisa Nunez
Robert C. O'Sullivan
Sandra Oberbroeckling
Andy Olson
Andrei Palamarchuk
Tanya Paperny
Jeffrey Warren Park
Galen Peiser
Sofia Perelygina
Mika Perkiömäki
Kathleen Peroff
Alexander Petrov
Tom Plummer
Yekaterina Polyakhova
Jon Powell
Noel Q.
Guy Ratki
Elizabeth Rattey
Tamara Real
Amy Reams
Nadia Repin
Paul Ricci
Helen Richardson
Jim and Kim Richardson
Trudy C. Ringer
Richard Rosing
Katherine L. Ross
Carol-Lynn Rössel
Hannah Rothman
Hope Rubin

Nelly Ruehl
Sharon Rusch
Jan Russak
Alison Ryland
Nadezhda Safyanik
R. Scheetz
Neala Schleuning, Ph.D.
Joerg Schwarzer
Shannon A. Scroggins
Donna T Seif
Christine M. Semenow
Tara Macias Serfaty
Sevenoaks School Russian Department, UK
John Shahan
Lizzie Shan
Jane Sharrow
Jane Robin Shaw
Yuliya Ivanovna Shulga
Carrie M. Simpson
Galina Skatkina
Jonathan C. Slaght
Ekaterina Slivko
Valentina Smith
Ina Sorokina
Linda J. Speck
Sally Baird Springer
Yulia Sribnaya
Dale and Mary Frances Stafford
M Stallion
Kristina Suderevskaya
Mary Sullivan
Anton Tarasenko
Thomas C. Taylor
Maria Tchelistcheff
Donald A. Thumim, Ph.D.
Konstantin and Maria Thurber
Glenn F. Tiedt
Eugenia Tietz-Sokolskaya
Catherine M Topolsky
John H Uhlemann
Alice Underwood
Charles Underwood
Tom & Olga Van Dis
Catherine Van Son
Konstantin Vanag
Iris van Veen
Ksenia Varlyguina
Evgeniya Vorontsova
Mark W
Richard Walker
Rieta Walker
Jacqueline Walker
Laura Walsh
Barbara Watson
Dawn Stuart Weinrraub
Kristen Welsh
Linda Wentworth
Tania Werbizky
Rita Antipov Whitney
Kevin Winter
Anastasia Wr
Richard Wright
Grigory Yaroshenko
Diana Yefanova
Olya Yurysheva
Katya Zalenskaya
Michael Zdanowski
Zoberano

SPECIAL THANKS

Aside from those who backed the project financially, and, of course, the amazing families of the centenarians, there were many who helped this project along its path, in many ways visible and invisible. At the risk of leaving someone out, here are all those to whom we wish to express a special measure of gratitude.

Rustem Adagamov
Katerina Afonchenkova
Ilya Agafonov
Irina Alashevich
Maria Antonova
Bob Barrett
Viktor Batkovich
Alexei Bayer
Elena Belyaeva
Natalia Beskhlebnaya
Brovchenko Family
Olga Chemerskaya
Olga Collin
Consulate of the Russian Embassy
Karen Dillon
Stanislav Dyakonov
Nuria Fatykhova
Alex Fegan
Irina Fomina
Darra Goldstein
Alexander Gontar
Victor Guadagno
Gulchachak
Olga Hauer-Tyukarkina
Heinrich-Böll-Stiftung
Emilia Kangasluoma
Sergey Karpov
Valeriya Karpova
Elsa Khoreva
Brendan Kiernan
Roman Korol and IVideos
Aleksei Kozlov
Ignat Kozlov
Robert Krattli
Olga Kravets
Dmitrij Lavrenko
Dmitry Lukyanenko
Nastasia Makarycheva
Lilit Matevosyan
Irina Mordasova

Peter Morley
Anar Movsumov
Jan Mukhamedzanov
Anna Nemtsova
Daria Ovechkina
PR of the Government of Tver region
Press Service of the Governor of Nizhny Novgorod region
Press Service of Kirov Rayon, St. Petersburg
Press Service of Krasnogvardey Rayonn, St. Petersburg
Ilya Rashkov
Stephanie Ratmeyer
Andrey Rubtsov
Nora Seligman Favorov
Stepan Serdiukov
Eileen Shine
Helga Shoshina
Irma Slepneva
Mikhail Solunin
Svetlana Sorokina
Marcin Stanowski
Taisia
Telegram Kanal @doskino
Nataliya Tochilenko
Daria Tomilova
Alexey Topolsky
Oleg Trofim
Anastasia Tsayder
Yulia Tsvyak
Suvi Turtiainen
Alice Underwood
Utka Veterans Council
Ilya Varlamov
Andrej Vasenyov
Sergey Vasilyev
Matti Vuorinen
Alexi Witwicki
Vladimir Yakovlev and "Vozrast Chastya"
Anisa Yanbaeva
Yasenevo Social Department, Administrative Department
Denise Youngblood
Andrei Zelenov